Praise for
Cool Mind Warm Heart

"Steve Roberts' essays display a courage found only in one who has attained a very personal and mercurial form of enlightenment. He surrounds our fears in unassailable love. Just Steve's wit and good humor makes them worth reading. I smile in wonderment."
> —*Odds Bodkin*, *Storyteller, Musician, and Author,*
> The Crane Wife

"If Cool Mind Warm Heart doesn't inspire one to go after and attain their heart's desire, I don't know what will. Steve Roberts looks at himself like nobody else I know. His honest self-reflection, self-depreciating humor and enduring hope made me smile in humble recognition."
> —*Janet McKenzie*, *Artist,*
> "Jesus of the People" —*Sister Wendy Beckett's choice*
> *for the new Millennium image of Jesus*

"Just when you believe you've considered every perspective—here comes Steve Roberts to kick down a new door with a hammer of love."
> —*Michael Jager*, *Founder, Partner,*
> Jager Di Paola Kemp Design, *Burlington, VT*

"Brilliant. We felt privileged just to be alive after reading just the first few pages of this passionate and deeply personal collection of essays."
> —*Craig and Patricia Neal*, *Founders,*
> Heartland Institute, *Edina, MN*

"Steve Roberts has the power to evoke a response in the reader which is both gentle and inviting. Who would think of writing about 'Why I love Alzheimers?' But that is part of his genius – to examine issues that confront all of us, find the value in the challenge and reframe it."

—*Mary McIsaac*, *Founder,*
The Center for Life Work and Planning, *Encinitas, CA*

"Knowing Steve Roberts is to know a person who lives his life in continual celebration, and the diversity of these essays will encourage the reader's own celebration of life."

—*John Ewing*, *Environmentalist, Lawyer, Founder,*
The Vermont Forum on Sprawl

"Steve Roberts is a man of Crazy Wisdom. His book illuminates the right questions—it is a pleasure to read."

—*Robert Perkins*, *Author,*
Talking to Angels, *Virgin, Utah*

"Steve Roberts' writing and wisdom are at once deep and humorous, profound and accessible. One essay put a soft smile on my face. The next created a big lump in my throat. Yet another had me thinking, simply: Wow. This is beautiful stuff. Very beautiful stuff."

—*Douglas Harp*, *Owner,*
Harp and Company, *Hanover, NH*
A fly-fishing, pond hockey-playing Buddhistly inclined, Harvard/Yale educated graphic designer who has always wanted to be on the cast of Saturday Night Live.

cool mind
warm heart

Cool Mind Warm Heart
Adventures with Life's Biggest Secret

Copyright © 2006 by Steve Roberts

ISBN 0-9767631-0-9

Library of Congress Control Number: 2005927479
CIP information available upon request

First Edition, 2006

St. Lynn's Press
POB 18680
Pittsburgh, PA 15236
412.466.0790
www.stlynnspress.com

Printed in the United States of America
on recycled paper 🔁

This title and all of St. Lynn's Press books may be purchased for educational, business, or sales promotional use. For information please write: Special Markets Department, St. Lynn's Press, POB 18680, Pittsburgh, PA 15236

10 9 8 7 6 5 4 3 2 1

cool mind
warm heart

adventures with life's biggest secret

everything is a gift

steve roberts

st. lynn's
press

PITTSBURGH

*Dedicated to the spirit of
Paramahansa Yogananda*

And to Dear, my beloved

Stagger onward rejoicing.

W. H. Auden

TABLE OF CONTENTS

Stories

Epilogue

INTRODUCTION

"You're nuts but you're welcome here."

O KAY, SO GOD SITS DOWN next to you and says, "It's your lucky day, my friend. I've come to tell you the secret of life."

What, in your view, will God say next?

If there is a right answer to this question, it's beyond me. But I do feel that each of us has our own answer.

After all, we make countless decisions every day based upon what we believe is real. Why else are we killing each other with such gusto in the name of righteousness? Why else do we get into spit-flying verbal fisticuffs over whether some movie or sports team is good or bad? Why else do I have a friend who swears that peanut butter prevents cancer? To put it rather grandly, each of us has our own view of how the universe operates.

Like everyone else, I have theories about things, lots of things. Theories, as you know, are just stories, things we make up to try and understand what's going on. One of my stories is that located at the core of our ego nature is a basic assumption we've latched onto that defines every choice we make. This assumption acts like a compass, ever orienting our fabrication of life. It also acts like a radio beacon—*beep, beep, beep*—and is therefore the overriding message we communicate to all we encounter. We may think we're expounding upon life, liberty and the pursuit of horse sense, or discussing why green eggs and ham is the world's best breakfast, or explaining how to master a fly fisher's flick of the wrist, but what we're really doing, moment by moment, is broadcasting our fundamental take on the secret of life.

Such as:

If you screw up, you're dead meat.

The universe is a friendly place.

You can never be too careful.

Things always turn out for the best.

We're all victims of circumstances beyond our control.

And so on.

Why mention this? It seems that any book with such an ambitious title as *Cool Mind Warm Heart* (the term Huston Smith used to describe the quintessence of the Buddha) ought to at least nod in the direction of life's master principle.

So here's my answer, my best shot at the secret the God of my imagination is hiding up Her sleeve: *Everything is a gift.*

Don't get me wrong. I'm not saying that an impending nuclear holocaust is reason to throw a luau (though, I must admit, that would be a healthier response than most, especially if what we're celebrating is beauty in the face of death). Of course pain and loss are real. The question is, what's their purpose? What's the purpose of everything?

My story is that every heartbreak, every joy, every moment, every circumstance is the universe calling us to open ourselves to the boundless love that is the essential vibration of existence. Robin Williams says that cocaine is God's way of telling us we have too much money. The spirit of that quip carries a lot of truth, in my experience. The universe is always talking to us, always encouraging us to make healthy choices, choices that serve our heart's desire for joy, or as a monk friend of mine calls it,"happiness on demand." As I see it, the blessing of addiction—whether our drug is cocaine or saving the world or hating people who've never been to a NASCAR race—is that it shows us the kinds of choices that won't get us where we want to go.

Pain, to me, is not punishment. Pain is the universe saying, "No, no, my child. Make another choice. You are much bigger than this. You are divine. Ultimately, you can make room for everything."

Making room is the practice of growing compassion. I doubt anything has been more difficult for me, maybe for anyone, given the horror we all experience personally and witness in the lives of others. And yet, for example, here's the Dalai Lama who considers many Chinese leaders to be among his most important teachers in this lifetime despite their intention to destroy the Tibetan people—an intention that has been carried out for decades through systematic murder, degradation, imprisonment and the imposition of inhumane laws.

We may smile at the Jewish proverb *"Love thy neighbor, even when he plays the trombone,"* but we know that to apply its deepest meaning takes almost inconceivable courage and commitment. And that is precisely its gift. Our elders remind us that growing old isn't for sissies, but is there a moment after conception when we're not growing old?

Some say it takes a million incarnations to become fully enlightened—to live in conscious union with all of existence. Believe it or not, I'd say many of us are well on our way.

My story is that for most of those million incarnations, we live in a manner that is little more than the equivalent of smashing our head against a brick wall. Then, along about life 900,000, give or take, we begin to realize that we're ending each incarnation with a massive headache.

"Hey, what's the deal?" we say. "There's got to be more than this."

With that, things start to shift. Sure, we still make insane choices, like blaming others for our anguish or deciding we're unworthy of happiness. But somewhere in us is this growing awareness that life's greatest gift is the gift of choice, and that our most important choice is love or fear.

Admittedly, it's a choice that can take a while to get the knack of. A hundred thousand lives, say. Yet all the while we're becoming more aware that life is a lot simpler than we had ever imagined. For one thing, we discover we don't need to change a thing—not others, and not us. All we need to do is love.

As I'm writing this, the remarkable Johnny Carson has died.

I can think of no other mortal whom we Americans, as a family, have turned to for sustenance so regularly, and for so long. Thirty years. Five times a week for more than 1500 weeks, totaling some 5000 hours of late-night television. The equivalent of 2500 motion pictures. Pundits are saying that "The Tonight Show" was as important for many adults as a nightly bedtime story is for a child. Johnny Carson's energy was what 10 to 15 million people at the end of their day chose to take with them into the dreamtime, that period of restoration at the core of our physical and emotional well-being. Why? Why were we so captivated by him? His humor gives us one clue. He skewered without mercy, but didn't demean. Steve Martin put his finger near the truth in his New York Times op-ed eulogy when he said, speaking to Carson directly, "You knew how to treat everyone." This is pretty high praise considering that Johnny's 23,000 guests included the full range of humanity from presidents to rodents, and the rodents might poop on his head. Martin wrote: "You gave each guest the benefit of the doubt, and in this way you exemplified an American ideal: You're nuts but you're welcome here."

If the secret of life is that everything is a gift, then its corollary—the secret of actually living, of manifesting our true selves—is welcoming everyone, nuts and all.

Making this practice a focus of every breath we take is the story of our spiritual journey over those million incarnations. No surprise it takes so long. Imagine living an entire day without blaming yourself or anyone else for anything. Yet that's pretty much all it takes to be a saint, so I'm told.

Is it any wonder that making room for differences is right up there with juggling refrigerators in the difficulty department? Or that "Everything is a gift" just may be the most fear-provoking possibility the world has ever known?

Anyway, that's my two cents. The surgeon who removed my prostate told me that in his 20 years behind the scalpel, I was the first person he'd met who called cancer a gift. So I'll certainly understand if you find my view of things a stretch.

The spirit of the universe, as I experience it, is playful, loving and deep. (I have this image of God continually whispering in our ear, "Now if I were you...and I am...") This book is my way of bowing to the love, depth and playfulness that lives in me, in you, and in whatever adventures of the soul we must have shared in previous lives to bring us together once again.

We all absorb meaning in ways that are far more subtle and mysterious than words alone can satisfy. Which is why, in addition to essays and stories, these pages include photographs of stone sculptures I've built on my farm. Stones, like words, have a life of their own. Both are teachers I revere, relentlessly prodding me to get out of my own way; although I must say that, so far, no word has rolled onto my fingers as many stones have—deliberately, if you ask me.

My feelings writing this introduction bring to mind a lovely old monk, long dead now, whose job was to train postulants in the ashram of an avatar. True story. This older monk and a bunch of his young charges are hanging out one day when one of the youngsters says, "Isn't it wonderful that we have the opportunity to be here, together, in this life, as devotees of a great master, an incarnation of God? It is a privilege. But it is also a great responsibility."

To which the old monk shakes his head and says, "No. It is only a privilege."

Sun Bear Farm
Valentine's Day, 2005

ESSAYS

BEING MOTHERED
BY STONES

It is said that you find two kinds of people on Everest: those who wish to climb her, and those who wish to stand on top.

IT DOESN'T TAKE MUCH for me to feel humble. After all, I wrestle stones. These jewels of the Vermont landscape remind me that life is a practice of bringing the kindest heart we can to every moment we have, and that to do so demands a very special relationship with the earth. Which may be why, to me, stones are like badgers: fearless, relentless. I've got the scars to prove it.

May 20, 2004 was among the deadliest days on Mt. Everest. Six people died, including some of the world's most experienced mountaineers. Those who reached the summit and lived to tell about it included one David Watson of Vermont.

In a subsequent interview Mr. Watson made it clear that he certainly hadn't "conquered" Everest. "I feel like I worked with the mountain, and she let me to the top. It's definitely a symbiotic relationship."

The Tibetans believe that Everest is the Mother Goddess of the World. David Watson has found that "...if you don't go there with a good heart and good intentions, you won't get to the top. You really have to be in tune with your heart and listen to the mountain."

Whatever else Everest may be, I feel she is a dramatic example of the sacred power that exists in the earth everywhere, and thus is available to each of us, not just mountain climbers. All we need do, as Mr. Watson says, is be in tune with our heart and listen.

My understanding of this practice has deepened since I became a wild man infatuated with building stone sculptures.

I fell in love with my bride pretty much the instant we met, and I fell in love with stones just about as quickly.

One day, for no particular reason, I started picking up and replacing the "droppings" that had tumbled from the many rock walls built on our land during the past two centuries. Next thing I know I've got a crowbar and a tractor with a bucket. I've worn out several dozen pair of work gloves. I'm schlepping boulders that can weigh more than a sumo wrestler, and I'm dotting our 200-acre mountainside with rock formations that suggest the artifacts of a prehistoric culture—or a fellow with definitely too much time on his hands. If I build all the sculptures I can imagine, just on this farm, I'll live to be at least 175. I'm like a man with a hammer in a nail factory.

Along the way, stones have become my teachers, and not just the ones that spark some pretty colorful epithets when they roll on my fingers or drop on my toes.

The inevitable despair that comes from trying to make a stone do something against its nature has led me to become a better listener, more fluid in letting go of preconceptions, and more able simply to be an instrument in service to something larger than myself.

But the biggest thing I've learned from stones is that to be a listener, to be fluid, to be an instrument doesn't happen by just thinking about it—I must also allow myself to be mothered by the earth, the ultimate nurturer.

I believe that those who say we can destroy the earth are mistaken. We can surely make the planet uninhabitable (we seem to be moving in that direction with mindless alacrity), but destroying the earth is something else again. Whether Hiroshima or Chernobyl or Mt. St. Helens, the earth heals her wounds relatively quickly. I have a feeling that if every nation detonated its entire stockpile of weapons and unleashed every poison possible, we humans might cease to exist, but some number of millennia down the road—hardly a blink in the universal scheme of things—Mother Earth herself would be thriving once again. The land is the mother that never dies, say the Maori.

Such is her resilience, her power, as well as the depth of her urging for us to live in conscious union with the Yin of creation. There's a reason we humans are making life increasingly miserable for ourselves, the same reason many die on Everest: lack of attunement.

Of course, awareness of this truth is one thing, action another—as I demonstrate regularly when some rock extravaganza about which I am oh-so-proud collapses with a noise that, to my ear, sounds suspiciously like a chuckle.

Among the spiritual practices I'm attempting to get the hang of is navigating my moments resting in the energetic embrace of the earth. From this grounded place, on those rare occasions I actually remember to choose it, an amazing thing happens. My mind lives in service of my heart, rather than the other way around. This shift is such a gift, for it means that I manage with a measure of grace, the fear and pain that arise in the natural course of events.

The big plan for my life is simply to

choose more of these moments.

It is said that you find two kinds of people on Everest: those who wish to climb her, and those who wish to stand on top. Both impulses are very much alive in each of us, I'd say: the ego's desire to win, and the heart's passion to join. The question is which do we ask to lead?

As my love affair with stones grows, so does the part of me that can make room for anything. It is an awakening that is not only beautiful but terrifying. Which is why, as powerful as the earth is, she's not more powerful than denial. I can ignore her with the best of them. I've got the scars to prove it.

THE HEART OF
SOCIAL RESPONSIBILITY

"Who will I be, or die trying?"

ONE DAY IN ST. MIKE'S grammar school, the parish priest gave a little talk about what a good thing it was for us kids to give to the collection basket every Sunday. I raised my hand and asked what if somebody gave a dollar infected with smallpox and the congregation died, would that still be a good thing? The poor padre thought I was being a wise guy, but I wasn't (well, maybe a little). Even then I must have sensed that behavior without consciousness was incomplete.

Among the many things we can celebrate

about humankind is our growing commitment to what is being called "social responsibility." Vermont has one of the nation's leading associations dedicated to this cause, Vermont Businesses for Social Responsibility. There are those who feel the U.S. constitution should be amended to incorporate a commitment to the principle. You could probably find a "socially responsible" approach to almost every human activity from conception to cremation, which may make this movement among the most powerful in the world's history. Still, "social responsibility" is a relatively new phenomenon, and so we continue to discover the depth of its meaning.

For instance, we are learning that social responsibility begins not with changing a single thing about the world, but rather with asking ourselves: Who am I committed to being?

We are learning that when we "make the world a better place" because we are angry, say, to pick a common motivation—what we're doing as much as anything else is perpetuating anger. And if that weren't enough, we are learning that making friends with anger (one of the indispensable steps toward actually managing it) may be harder than quelling terrorism or feeding the third of the world's population that goes to bed hungry every night. How many of us would rather chop off our hand than give up our attachment to righteous indignation? How many of us light a candle for the planet while we hate those goddamn polluters?

When the Dalai Lama met a Tibetan monk who had been imprisoned and tortured by the Chinese for several years, His Holiness asked the monk if he had been afraid. The monk replied, "My only fear was that I wouldn't have compassion for my captors." We do ourselves a disservice if we think of this monk as somebody special. He's just a guy trying to live the best life he knows how, like any of us. He knows that his life is not about his captors (the world outside of him), it is about himself— about who he is committed to being, regardless of anything else.

A company here in Vermont has taken the

courageous step of naming itself Seventh Generation, bowing to the Native American principle of making decisions with the awareness of our place at the center of a continuum that spans three generations before us and three generations after. This principle is especially powerful because it is impossible to know specifically how to realize it. Its value stems from how much the attempt to see our choices in a larger context becomes a conscious practice by every person who contributes to the organization's well being.

A friend of mine occasionally solicits my two cents about a non-profit he founded. His firm's aspirations are noble, their accomplishments admirable. But my friend looks at me a little askance when I say that I would serve their worst enemy with the same commitment I offer him and his team: to help them bring an ever-increasing awareness of who they are and who they can become to every choice they make.

Today, we are learning that the measure of health, whether of an individual or the planet, is defined primarily by one thing: Resilience—the ability to respond in a positive way to any eventuality.

A healthy enterprise, then, like a healthy person, is one engaged in a never-ending assessment of those fundamental questions of purpose, values, and goals—and from that assessment, linking commitments to action. The key modifier here is "never-ending."

It was a different though equally well-intentioned priest who, at my father's wake, made the offhand remark that we are all sinners. I was 27. Speak for yourself, I said to him. Are you saying you've never sinned? he asked. Oh no, Father, I said. You name it, and I'm sure I've either done it or wanted to. But I've also played a lot of basketball, and I don't consider myself a basketball player.

As we grow in our understanding of what it takes to be socially responsible, we are learning that organizations that stagnate or die do so, at least in part, because they have neglected to address who they truly are. Their focus is primarily external, rather than within. Many of us who live lives of quiet desperation, as Thoreau calls it, do so for the same reason— shying away from the question that lies at the heart of not only social responsibility, but of life itself: Who will I be or die trying?

RUTHLESS SAINTS

*Given the choice of spending Christmas with
Christ or Hanukkah with Hitler,
a ruthless saint might opt for the latter. . .*

H ERE'S ONE MEASURE of how the world
is heading in a positive direction.

Fifty years ago the epitome of the circus
was Ringling Brothers and Barnum & Bailey.
With its lion tamers, dancing bears, trick horses, performing elephants, monkeys on bikes,
and seals bouncing beach balls on their noses,
the implicit message was "Man Over Beast."
Even the aerialists, tightrope walkers, jugglers,
fire-eaters, knife-throwers and human pretzels

were an example of "Man Over the Beast Within."

Today, the epitome of the circus is Cirque du Soleil. Its implicit message is "The Celebration of Humanity." Indeed, Cirque leaves most churches in the dust when it comes to inspiring the integration of body, mind and spirit—the criteria for living as a whole person.

I find it revealing to play the game, "If I Were a (fill in the blank)." If I were an automobile, I'd be a 1957 Chevrolet convertible, black with a fiery red interior. Maybe in every man there is a teenage boy still lusting for those wheels that first represented both the fullness of his spirit and the emptiness of his purse.

If I were a woman from another era, I'd be Sojourner Truth, who, come to think of it, was herself black with a fiery red interior. An illiterate slave powered by a fierce relationship with the divine, she became one of the most inspiring and influential citizens of 19th century America.

And, if I were a present-day organization of any kind, I would actually be two: Alcoholics Anonymous and Cirque du Soleil.

AA is a story for another time, except to say that it is among the most important fellowships on earth, since addiction is at the heart of much, if not all, human misery. Alcohol is merely one of its more deadly expressions. Others include power, beliefs, anger, work, play, eating and blame. AA is a useful benchmark for those who would recover from any addiction. In fact, it's just possible that AA's operating principles are up there with the Declaration of Independence as an inspired framework for human liberation. The proof of AA's power is found solely in the millions of people it helps to live sober—one day at a time.

The proof of Cirque's power, to me anyway, is that I can't watch it without crying.

Here are hundreds of the planet's most exceptional performers and everyone who gives them life, all striving to convey a vision of dignity, joy, depth, a world without limits, jubilation, playfulness, breaking the bonds of ignorance, overcoming indifference, etcetera, etcetera—and, needing to open themselves perhaps more completely than they ever imagined possible in order to even approach pulling it off.

Of all the reasons we love a circus, perhaps none is more indelible than those moments when we find ourselves, heart in mouth, wondering, "How did they ever do that?" Cirque du Soleil is masterful at arousing our imagination to ask that question time and again, as if Cirque's only mantra were the one I've known a saint to use: more and better. And now, the spirit of that mantra has given birth to programs created by people who are, you might say, "offspring" of Cirque de Soleil. One of them is Normand Latourelle, architect of the astonishing *Cavalia: A Magical Encounter Between Man and Horse.*

Cavalia (which took six years and $27 million to create before opening in 2003) is a spectacle of myth, magic and poetry, as if a dream from our childhood has suddenly and all-but-unbelievably come to life, involving *Lord of the*

Rings costumes, daring acrobatics, original music, projected images and more than 60 performers, half of them horses.

The human/horse relationship in *Cavalia* is as far removed from the historic "show 'em who's boss" philosophy of training as a duck is from a dill pickle.

Kindness, trust and positive reinforcement are what persuade mature stallions to work together in total freedom—without a trace of tack—in the presence of lighting, music, and more than 1800 spectators, as the horses' human partners leap on and off them in ways only world-class gymnasts can.

All the while, the universe is beating its drum, calling us all: "Ho! This unfathomable beauty is who you really are."

Although you wouldn't necessarily know it by the barbaric choices we humans make every day in the name of goodness, our collective evolution over the past few thousand years has been a continual, and actually relatively speedy, awakening of consciousness.

According to a monk friend of mine, about 1500 years before Jesus, Moses preached an idea revolutionary for the time: "Don't kill your brother." When Jesus came along, he advised something that was, for his time, equally radical: "Love your brother." Today, we're gulping at another notion: "You *are* your brother." That's a pretty big shift in just 3500 years, but such is the nature of our unfolding.

Cirque du Soleil is an example of life near the leading edge of that unfolding. Yet Cirque is not unique. Many organizations are home to people I like to call ruthless saints. Given the choice of spending Christmas with Christ or Hanukkah with Hitler, a ruthless saint might opt for the latter, not because he or she feels that Hitler is God-like, but because lighting the menorah with the Führer would oblige them to grow their love much more than singing Silent Night with the Prince of Peace.

Ruthless saints are men and women engaged in a practice of deepening their attunement to the unconditional possibility of the universe. They are uncompromising in assessing the extent to which their life expresses that attunement. One sign on their fridge says, "No Blame." Another says, "Everyone is Our Teacher."

The growing number of ruthless saints is the real proof that the world is moving in a positive direction. And the best news is you might meet one anywhere.

In the mirror, for instance.

LEARNING AT THE SPEED OF FEAR

Fear is one of the greatest teachers on earth, up there with Jesus and Buddha.

THE REQUEST CAME in August 2001, a month before September 11th: The coming October, would I please give a keynote address about making one's professional life fun. In the aftershock of the terrorist attacks, my hosts hastily called back to say that perhaps a different topic would be better suited to the nation's mood. I said actually I was feeling just the opposite, since, in my experience, what it takes to have fun is precisely what it takes to handle a profound emotional upheaval.

Fun (as I know it) is the ability to influence our environment, to shape the circumstances in which we find ourselves. If we cannot do that, life is anything but enjoyable. And the most significant influence we can have—the only *meaningful* influence, really—is the extent to which we can manage ourselves. The more we are able to manage us, and therefore the more resilience and peace we bring to our moments, the more options we have in our interactions with the world. And options are the lifeblood of fun.

If, for instance, we feel overwhelmed by another's anger, we may feel we have no options other than enduring, running, or attacking—none of which falls into the fun zone.

But if, in the presence of another's anger, we are able to become energetically big enough so that the person's fear (for that's what anger is, underneath), as well as our own, washes through us—then we experience the kind of joy that comes from being present, pliant and loving regardless of the external circumstance.

That joy, curiously enough, is the biggest gift we can offer another human being.

Basically then, fun is the direct result of managing fear.

And here, wouldn't you know, is where things get a little sticky.

Fear may be the most offensive four-letter word in American business. It can be easier to admit our predilection for naked bowling than to admit we're afraid. Somehow we have this belief that fear is bad, weak, disgusting, inappropriate, unmanly, whatever. Even some consultants who say they help organizations manage fear use language like "driving fear from the workplace." Sadly, that language itself is fear-driven. We see fear as an enemy, something to be destroyed, which actually makes us puppets of fear. It is ironic, though hardly amusing, that we have a hostile relationship with what is perhaps the most pervasive influence in our life.

But it won't always be this way. Here are some basics about fear that we are beginning to appreciate:

Fear is an everyday, ordinary part of us—very much like our height, weight, flat feet, beautiful nose and addiction to chocolate. In other words, fear is human, and therefore sacred. It exists to serve us. It is not the bogeyman.

Fear is one of the greatest teachers on earth, up there with Jesus and Buddha, because in every moment fear shows us what we must address in order to be who we really are: a being of kindness. That's why fear is known as the golden key that unlocks the heart. My fantasy is that a few thousand years from now, when we humans are a bit more spiritually grown-up, we will actually celebrate a national holiday of fear, kind of like Valentine's Day. Or maybe that's what Halloween will become: A reminder to be aware of all the masks we wear in life because we fear being ourselves.

Our honoring of fear will emerge as we learn how fear unmanaged acts as a governor, limiting our ability to embrace the vastness of who we are. To the extent that we choose not to move through fear, to continually let it flow from us rather than hold on to it, that is the extent to which we choose to be imprisoned by our ignorance, our beliefs, our preferences, our habits, our rules, our addictions—and all the other constructs of the ego.

Love, we are discovering, is much more than an emotion. It is also an action. And the action is letting go of fear. Love blossoms as fear is released—and not released harshly as if we are expelling some demon, but released lovingly, with gratitude for all that the fear has taught us. That's about all there is to being a healthy human being: Recognize fear, feel it, let it go, then attune ourselves ever more deeply to the love that fear has masked, the love that has always burned within us.

Courage, we find, is not the opposite of fear. Courage is the practice of learning at the speed of fear, meeting fear instantly, with open arms and an open heart.

In a book I cannot recall is the sentence: *God comes when the vessel is empty.* We don't have to believe in a Higher Power to experience the truth of this sentiment. As we allow fear to flow through us, the inevitable result is greater pliancy and resilience. And with plian-cy and resilience comes joy—another name for fun.

WHY I LOVE ALZHEIMER'S

My mother and I would sit together for hours without talking, and yet the "conversation" we shared felt in my heart like the one we must have had when I was in her womb.

M Y MOTHER DIED of Alzheimer's. My mother-in-law, mother to me in more ways than marriage, has been in the disease's complete rapture for a few years now. My father-in-law, another source of light during the 30 years his daughter and I have been partners, recently died with his mind able to recall only the briefest bits of the previous ten minutes. These three elders are nobody special in the world of dementia, but through them I have become aware of how young we humans are when it comes to communicating with one another at the most fundamental level—heart to heart, or essence-to-essence. This makes Alzheimer's an invaluable teacher. Not a popular one, to be sure. Watching a loved one's mind gradually disappear is an excruciating transition for those of us who consider intellect the measure of personhood. Yet, within the pain of this loss is, I feel, the call of the universe to open ourselves to the possibility that maybe we're missing something—that maybe there are ways of connecting that are more real than a robust dialogue or a funny story or a small piece of wisdom, or even the ability to state our own name. I, for one, have found that there are.

Recently I heard a lovely anecdote about an elderly man who, every morning at a certain time, stopped whatever he was doing so that he could run off to an appointment. When asked by someone who didn't know him all that well what was so compelling, the man said, "My wife has Alzheimer's. She's in a nursing home, and we have a daily date for lunch."

"Isn't it wonderful that your wife still knows who you are?" the person said.

"Oh, she doesn't at all," the elderly man said, "but I know who she is."

It's a heartwarming story, but there is a kernel of it that eludes my own experience. When the man says he knows who his wife is, what I feel he's really saying is that he knows who he remembers her being, beyond the various roles of lover, mother, friend, et al. Fair enough. But I wonder if there is a part of his wife that the man has yet to meet, for if he did he would know that, indeed, she *does* know who he is—just not on any terms he is familiar with.

My mother and I would sit together for hours without talking, and yet the "conversation" we shared felt in my heart like the one we must have had when I was in her womb. Or maybe it was the resonance that evolves between two people who have known each other over any number of incarnations. Talk about something that's hard to put into words, much less to comprehend on any "normal" terms. Yet, in my mother's presence, I learned that if I gave up thinking or needing or wanting or judging and just showed up with an open heart willing to experience and participate in whatever might present itself, magic would happen. I would feel an innate, timeless connection to all of existence and the ever-new, depthless and unconditional support that infuses that connection regardless of pain or fear or suffering. And that feeling might arise as I was changing her diaper just as easily as when she would unexpectedly put her hand on my cheek.

When, a few years later, the inner world of my in-laws became overwhelmingly surreal, I felt the universe once again demanding that I do my best to give up every belief and expectation about how life is or ought to be, and simply bring as much love as I could to each moment. One outcome was the afternoon my father-in-law and I drove from Vermont to Boston and had the exact same conversation, brand new, at least 25 times—and through this, on some cellular level, became simply two guys who loved each other out on a grand adventure. If, in the great beyond we're invited to name the top 10 experiences of our life, I suspect both of us might include that ride.

There are those who say that the biggest challenge facing humankind is our difficulty in making room for differences. Alzheimer's can show us how true that is. I can't count how many times my own unmanaged fear has prompted me to wish that the elders in my life with Alzheimer's would die. I do know one thing: It's not as many times as I've been grateful for all that they've taught me about how to love.

THE PART OF ME
THAT IS BLACK

*Those women have deepened my awareness
of many things, rage and reverence among them.
Go beyond awareness, they also call.
Make choices.*

I WATCHED Dr. Martin Luther King's "I Have a Dream" speech live on television—the sole white person, boy of 19, among a dozen black cleaning ladies in Fayetteville, North Carolina—and you can believe those women were talking to the TV: Their shouts, their tears, their Amens & Halleluiahs, their curses, their laughter...inflamed by passions centuries in the making. I felt witness to an ancient tribal ceremony. I'd been an altar boy in grammar school. I spent most of high school in a seminary. Solemn I knew. But what I had never known was a gathering so sacred.

I have had almost no association with African-Americans day-to-day, or people of any color for that matter. Yet African-Americans in particular have played a role in a number of events—more than I can recount here—that continue to shape who I am. That afternoon in the day room of a Fort Bragg officer's quarters was one. Over the years those women have deepened my awareness of many things, rage and reverence among them. Go beyond awareness, they also call. Make choices.

I grew up outside a small village in the Finger Lakes of New York State. Until I entered the Army I'm not sure I ever met a black person. The next event I'm about to relate occurred in 1955. September.

I'd be turning 12 in a couple of months. My dad had just bought a brand new gray and white '56 Ford Fairlane, frilled with chrome and budding fins. He could have driven home the Taj Mahal and I wouldn't have been more impressed. I admired my dad. He played catch with me almost every day spring and summer. He took me to Yankee Stadium. He told me I could do anything. He was a Phila-delphia butcher's boy who had made himself a successful stock broker until the crash of '29. Broke, he worked his way to Europe on a freighter where he spent the Depression living off his wits. On two occasions when he was past the age of 40, my father moved his family across the country even though he had no work waiting for him. His confidence has inspired me on many occasions. The first move, from Long Island to Phoenix, was intended to give my mother's sinus condition a friendlier cli-mate. The second, from Phoenix to the Finger Lakes, was to buy the farm he and my mom had always dreamed of owning. I was eight when we arrived in one of the most gorgeous but economically depressed counties of New York. There must have been some pretty frugal times, but I was not aware of them. When my father died 20 years later, my mother, a homemaker who lived another three decades, never knew a moment of financial insecurity.

After supper we take the maiden family cruise in the new 'mobile. At one point we stop at the red light in the center of town. As we sit there, quiet, proudly conspicuous (speaking for myself), a sensational brand new green and gold Dodge, the equal of our Ford in embellishments, illuminated by that rich Hollywood evening sun that happens only in September, passes before us on the crossing street, captivating our attention as if it were an ocean liner. Inside the car is a family just like ours: mom and dad and some kids. The family is black. As the Dodge disappears, from the stillness my father says, "I wonder where a nigger got the money to buy a car like that."

In the echo of that remark my childhood began to end. I met my father as simply a man afraid, among all his other qualities. And for some reason I felt for the first time the harm inflicted on the whole of creation anytime we consider someone else as "the other."

A smart and delightful woman of African-American lineage, with whom I was in love for a few years in my 20's, is the reason that, at 27, I became the oldest freshman Amherst College had ever admitted. She and I met at a Boston radio and TV station where we worked. She had recently graduated from Smith. She said why don't you think about going to college? I said, well, I have always loved learning but I've never enjoyed school. She said maybe you've just never known a really good one, which was true. So I took some trips, visited schools that reject just about everybody, and was so impressed that I began a year-long campaign to get admitted to one of them. I felt like Don Quixote. I said to my friend you know I graduated next-to-last in my high school class. She said don't worry about it, it wasn't because you were dumb. You've got something going on in there. For one thing, you're about the least prejudiced white person I know.

As if the universe just couldn't wait to square that remark, not long after it I'm walking down a busy Boston street in broad daylight and hear running footsteps slapping up the sidewalk behind me. I look over my shoulder and see a teenage boy ordinary to my eye in every respect but the darkness of his skin. Terror ignites my blood.

The boy passed in and out of my vision in little more time than it takes to say so, but he has remained one of my teachers. If he'd been white, I'd have hardly noticed him. I was ashamed. More than 30 years later, that kid is still reminding me to be aware of ways in which fear of "the other" lives in me in any of its countless forms. Go beyond awareness, he also calls. Make choices.

SUPPOSE JESUS HAD BEEN MOLESTED BY A PRIEST

*It is fear that underlies the harmful choices
that certain priests have made.
And it is fear that underlies any reaction to
them other than love.*

THE GIFT OF ADVERSITY is that it helps to reveal who we really are. For Christians, one would presume, adversity is a rich opportunity to reaffirm, even celebrate, what it means to be "a follower of Jesus." And the nice thing is, being a disciple of Jesus can help one navigate life's vicissitudes with a single (though not always easy to use) question: *What would Jesus do?* Is there a circumstance to which that question is not a useful guide to a

Christian's life? I can't think of one: You spill grape juice on your dress; your dog eats your homework; you're abducted by aliens; you win the lottery—yada-yada.

The revelation of pedophile priests within the Catholic Church, then, is not fundamentally different from any other life event, spiritually speaking. For Catholics and other Christians it is an opportunity to gain an ever-deeper awareness for *What would Jesus do?*

And it isn't just lovers of Jesus for whom pedophile priests are powerful teachers. The many stories of this drama can help to awaken in each of us the extent to which we choose fear (or its cousins anger, blame, judgment, banishment, revenge, and righteousness, among others) over love. Whether any of these is what Jesus or any being we revere would choose, we must answer for ourselves. All of us can appreciate what is really being asked by the question: *Suppose Jesus had been molested by a priest. What would He do?*

It's easy to boil down Jesus's teachings to a couple of words. Two of my favorites are love and forgiveness. Much harder is opening our hearts to the meaning of those actions, particularly when so many moments are full of pain.

The pedophile priest situation, deep with anguish for all concerned, is not unique. Every human has experienced many situations rife with heartbreak. But it isn't the situations themselves that matter—a failed marriage; a lost job; drug addiction; cancer; death; betrayal in any of its many forms; September 11—it is our response that reveals our willingness to love in that moment. Which is to say, we continually make the choice: love or fear.

As I see it, the Catholic Church has two primary functions. One, to preserve the integrity of what it feels are Jesus's teachings. And two, to be a role model for living those teachings. There is a legendary car salesman named Joe Girard. He's sold more cars than anyone on earth, supposedly, and his customers think he's terrific. Joe's been known to say, "If somehow I sell you a lemon, I'll be sorry, but I'll also be glad that I can show you how great our service department is." This is the attitude that any healthy person or organization has. I have no idea how well the Catholic Church preserves the integrity of Jesus's teachings, but as far as being a role model of health in response to the news of their troubled brothers, I'm not sure its clergy have always been as inspiring as they could be about the quality of their service department.

I'm not pointing fingers at the Church. The lives of its leaders are no different than the lives of its members, or the lives of any of us. We all know how difficult it is to live up to our own ideals. To expect a priest, or even the pope, to be fundamentally different from ourselves is to deny the oneness of the human family—indeed, the oneness of all life. Thinking we're different from someone else (or that they're different from us) is just another way we put fear in charge of our moments. It is fear that underlies the harmful choices that certain priests have made. And it is fear that underlies any reaction to them other than love.

Regardless of anyone else's choices, each of us can use this whole pedophile priest business to strengthen our own relationship with our self. We can go within and ask: *How do I run from answering the call of my heart to love?*

Put another way, we don't need to be a Christian to find it helpful in any moment to wonder: *What choice would Jesus make, right here, right now?*

IT BREAKS MY HEART
TO VOTE

As George Carlin says, we're a great country, but a strange culture.

M Y SON PETER became a bank robber so that he wouldn't die from his addiction to crack. Robbing a bank was the only way he knew to get himself off the street and off the pipe. His options, as he saw them, were jail or death.

Such is the power of despair.

I hired a lawyer for him. Fortunately, Peter was a first-time offender who had carried no weapon and didn't threaten anyone. Prosecutors see guys like him all the time: technically a criminal; in reality, a drug addict. The lawyer negotiated a deal where, instead of hard time, Peter was sentenced to a six-month drug rehab "boot camp." He completed the "boot camp" and was paroled. Within a few weeks he started using again, and to support his habit robbed another bank.

Such is the power of addiction.

This time I hired no lawyer. Being a recovering alcoholic myself, I knew that things often have to get worse before there is even a chance they'll get better. Few choices have been more painful than surrendering the desire to intervene on behalf of my child. All I can do is be present and loving as Peter makes his own choice to live or die. To be present means, among other things, not holding on to the past or having expectations about the future. And the only way I can really be present, and love, is to forgive myself for the times when my addictions have killed my life.

What does this have to do with voting?

I feel the same way about my nation as I feel about my son. It is a pain that is especially acute when it comes to electing a president. As George Carlin says, we're a great country, but a strange culture. It breaks my heart to vote. Part of me feels that no matter who I vote for, I am basically enabling our cultural addiction to blame, intolerance and denial. I feel that, to a far greater degree than is useful, the left and right of American politics are two sides of the same coin called bigot. To me, a bigot is someone who makes no room for another.

As a result, we give birth to presidential candidates whose primary quality is not the ability to bring forth the inherent greatness of America's diversity, but to pander to our addictions: Our addiction to seeing the world simplistically. Our addiction to blaming others for our pain. Our addiction to denying the connectedness of everyone on the planet. Our addiction to the belief that it is possible to create a "safe" world without growing our capacity to love. To name just a few.

How could it be otherwise? Our presidents are merely reflections of ourselves.

I pray that my son reaches a place of such utter despair that he says, "I will do anything never to be here again." I just hope that, should he say it, it isn't with his dying breath. Likewise, I pray that we as a culture will awaken ever more fully to the harm caused by our addictions—and do so before freedom and equality are considered luxuries.

It breaks my heart that my vote is construed as support for a particular candidate or ideology.

In 2004, when Bruce Springsteen and friends kicked off the "Vote for Change" tour, they said, "We're here tonight to fight for a government that is open, rational, forward-looking and humane, and we're going to rock the joint while doing so." That's what I'd like my vote to stand for—including the rock the joint part—but unlike Mr. Springsteen, I don't feel that, as a culture, we create presidential candidates who can actually be the agent of such inspired common sense. Not at the moment, anyway.

I vote for what may seem a very strange reason. The pain of it reminds me that making America healthier is only incidentally about who is president, and absolutely about who am I. As Gandhi says, we must be the change we wish to bring about in others. Only by forgiving myself for the ways in which my own addictions have harmed me and others can I truly serve my nation—by being present and loving regardless of the insane choices we all contribute to.

KNOWING YOU'RE GOING TO BE HANGED IN THE MORNING

I suffer from the most extreme form of insanity
the world has ever known:
I live in heaven, and I complain.

W HEN I AWOKE after the operation, for a few seconds I couldn't tell whether I was alive or not. I mean physically. Anesthesia can do that: create a jump-cut in time and space; and your mind's knee-jerk reaction is to assess if this shift is *The Big Shift*. I was disoriented, curious, but not particularly afraid. Nor have I been surprised since to have the experience repeat itself—momentary slips into the void. And now, beyond these brief wrinkles in time, something else is happening. My being, while at rest in the dreamtime, is occasionally chauffeured to an unfamiliar but wholly welcome dimension where my cells swoon at the caress of divine mothering. Unconditional love, unconditional acceptance, a heightened awareness of the present (past and future having fallen away), and not least of all a kind of voiceless guidance that seeps as if by osmosis into every neutron so that I open my eyes a different person. They say our body replaces 100 percent of its cells every seven years. Sometimes I feel as though mine are being, not replaced exactly but *overhauled*, scrub-a-dub-dubbed, every seven minutes. I know what's going on. I am being "taught." Continual surrender of every smidgeon of identity manufactured by my ego is a choice I must make, new and passionately, every moment. I also know that these heavenly kisses of illumination, along with the surgery itself and everything around it, represent another phase of my spiritual journey—revealing to me more of what must be joyfully cremated in the fire of love as I learn to live consciously in the lap of Spirit. I am sympathetic to anyone who finds this a bit strange. *Gift* is not usually the first thing that pops to mind when we hear the word *cancer*.

The rather limited ability of us humans at this point in our evolution to manage fear leads us to create beliefs that are astonishingly restrictive. We have an intense list of things that are desirable, and maybe an even more intense list of things that aren't. And as far as what's right, real, appropriate, worthy, ridiculous or evil is concerned, we may not have all the answers, but we're almost never lacking in an opinion. Fear does that, keeps us scrambling compulsively to create external safety in whatever forms we can: laws, rules, plans, dress-codes, diets, fashions, fitness, academic pedigrees, even flag waving—not in service of our heart's call for *Unity*, but in reaction to our ego's terror of vulnerability. I am humbled by the human capacity for selflessness, and the extraordinary beauty we are capable of creating. Yet, our everyday behavior as a species suggests that, in some respects, we're not all that far along in our evolution. We can still look over our shoulder and see the cave. What reason other than an infantile fear of the unknown leads us to perpetuate discrimination of any kind, from sticking up our nose at another's hairstyle to genocide? No mature person needs to degrade another in order to feel secure. The Germans didn't kill Jews because they felt Jews were inferior. That story only demonstrates how masterful we humans are at rationalization. The Holocaust took place because enough Germans felt inadequate in themselves. Like the bully on the grammar school playground who goes around knocking other kids into the mud while saying, "See, I'm better than you." My point, to be sure, is not Germans. Sadly, perhaps the only thing unusual about the Holocaust is the numbers, the conspicuous violence, not the conscious intent to harm, or the extent to which we deny the harm we do. That happens all the time, all over the globe. At this point in our evolution, we judge, ostracize, condemn, banish, annihilate, and otherwise deny the existence of others as if the practice were something we needed for survival, like air or food. (As I write this, America is at war with Iraq. The "rightness" of the war aside, why do you suppose that virtually no mainstream American media, much less the government, reports on the devastation this war is causing to Iraqi civilians? Why do we turn our collective heads from the carnage we are choosing to inflict? I'll bet at least one reason is similar to why we might decline to watch a video of a steer in a slaughterhouse being dispatched and butchered before we cut into a juicy slice of him on our dinner plate). I think of us as children playing grownup, although by no means do I imply the benign pleasure of pretending we're Spiderman or Cinderella. On the other hand, we're not evil or flawed or any nonsense like that. We're just young. Anyone who believes that he or she is either superior or inferior to another human being for any reason—brains, money, integrity, blood, nationality, religion—is, in my estimation, a child: ignorant. Which includes just about all of us this side of sainthood. But hey, the fact that we're children means we're growing up. Come back and visit in a few thousand years.

Today, even the desire for "harmony" usually springs from fear: the urge to keep life smooth so that we circumvent any challenges to our ego's sense of security—no messy tête-à-têtes, thank you. Meanwhile, life passes by largely unappreciated, virtually all of its marrow intact, because we've already made up our mind what it's all about, usually down to the smallest, silliest detail: *Spending your birthday in the hospital is unpleasant; cold applesauce is better than warm*—being just two of the beliefs tossed my way in post-op with all the best of intentions by those who nursed me. We're a bit like the pickpocket who, even in the presence of a grizzly bear in a tuxedo, sees only pockets. At its core, our inability to manage fear causes us to ignore one of the few spiritual truths worth paying attention to: that One Life pervades everything, as Paramahansa Yogananda put it. To awaken from the illusion of separateness is life's purpose, says Thich Nhat Hanh. Is there a more foreign idea to humankind today than "everything is a gift"? No wonder so many of us believe that cancer is bad news.

Why do I feel differently?

I suffer from the most extreme form of insanity the world has ever known: I live in heaven, and I complain.

That may seem like a non-sequitur from a guy who isn't grousing about his cancer—but leave us not forget that life is a superstore of opportunities to find the universe lacking. I almost always have one or more items in my shopping cart. Don't we all? One of my favorite movie directors, John Waters, says he could never be friends with a man who wears white bucks out of season, a rather curious prejudice for a fellow who has made "tasteless" an art form. My hot button is whiners, people who consider themselves victims. If it weren't for them, I'd be happy.

I was born "knowing" that the universe was a friendly place, a place of nurturance, a place that, while including incomprehensible darkness, was, on the whole, inherently benevolent—not just for me but for everyone. The best singer for children I've ever heard, Red Grammar, has a song that says on the day we were born the angels sang and blew on their horns. That chorus reminds me of the Divine Presence I have experienced my whole life, a Presence that, when I choose to feel it, is not dissimilar to the joy of napping on my father's chest when I was a toddler. Yet, like many of us I'm sure, I have too frequently ignored that Presence, allowing my attention to focus instead on the concerns or delights of my small self, my ego—the part of us that is a great servant but a piss-poor leader, adept at masterminding our expedition to the stars, but incapable of telling us whether it is right action to go there, a job only the heart can handle.

Tops among the various fears that define my life is surrendering all to Spirit—holding on not even to the wish for Oneness. Yet, my desire to surrender, to awaken from the illusion of separation, to be completely present here and now, is, in my heart of hearts, my passion, my life's intention. (There are those who say it is the passion of every heart, and that the story of our countless lives is the story of how that passion grows in us, cell by cell if you will, until we are completely consumed by its fire and light.) And since we get what we ask for, my intention draws to me with mathematical precision those circumstances that put me face-to-face with whatever stands between me and Oneness. In a word, control.

I don't mean for this to sound like a big revelation. After all, the vow of obedience in most religious orders originates from the truth that living in the Oneness of Spirit is to live in the void of no control. *If you can't surrender to the will of Brother Blah-Blah, whose management style is modeled on Blackbeard the Pirate, how can you possibly surrender to God? Surrendering on your terms is an oxymoron.* But the spirit of that drill is not unique to religious life. It is the request made of each of us all the time. It is the essential drama of existence: *Surrender (make room for) this, now this, now this...whatever separates you from any part of life.* Heck, the purpose of death is to remind us that letting go of our attachment to everything is the ticket to joy.

As we rev our passion for unity, it doesn't take long for things to get really hairy. We learn something terrifying: The purpose of life is not to love Buddha, or Jesus, or Mohammed, our guru, or our favorite saint or sage. Love and reverence and all that is fine, great, good, lovely, and helpful to be sure, but it's not the point. It's not the purpose of life. The purpose of life is to *become* Buddha or Jesus or Mohammed, et al—to cut through all our notions that there is a scintilla's difference between us and them, or between us and anybody for that matter. The primary reason there is even such an entity as Jesus or Buddha in the universe is to remind us of the consciousness we can, and will, attain sooner or later, as soon as we become masters of loving ourselves all the time, of forgiving ourselves for anything, and of letting go of fear, which includes letting go of beliefs, especially our most cherished ones, the beliefs we hold onto with ferocity. Stuff like: "I must be an honorable person," or "I'll never be enough," or "God is important in my life." They weigh a ton, if we're "serious" about them, whereas Oneness doesn't weigh a thing. Holding on to beliefs takes enormous energy, wearing us out, whereas Oneness means just that: We don't hold onto anything since we are already at one with all the energy of the universe.

Sooner or later we must lovingly bid all our beliefs good day. Few prospects are more frightening. The constructs of important/unimportant or honorable/dishonorable and the like are just polarities our ego makes up to feel *safe*, to be on the *right* side of things, to have *control*. The God of my heart is beyond all beliefs, beyond all ego-created notions of safety. God is only love, *only* being the operative word. God transcends any definition of love the mind can create. Love is the essential "stuff" of the universe; it makes up everything, including what and who we hate the most. There may be evil, but that too is God (since *only love* means just that—or as some saint said, "The devil knows not for whom he works"), showing us all the seductions we must embrace on our journey of inevitable reunion with

Spirit: the drop of the sea rejoining the ocean itself. "When you learn to love hell, you'll be in heaven," writes Thaddeus Golas in *The Lazy Man's Guide to Enlightenment*. Not only do I agree, but I say we're all going to heaven whether we like it or not, if not in this life then in another. (Or, as Edgar Cayce put it, "We don't go to heaven. We grow to heaven.") Spiritual awakening, if there is such a thing, may be no more than a process of becoming increasingly aware of the ways in which control, the ego's fear of vulnerability, shows up—and then of loosening its grip, eventually giving up control completely, living in the void of being.

Here's a mundane example. There are squirrels running around our yard, burrowing in to our various outbuildings for the winter, competing with the birds at the plethora of feeders we keep stocked like a buffet at the Ritz. My ego is afraid that the squirrels will get inside the house or my office and do some damage. My desire is to trap the squirrels and relocate them. But doing so at this time of year (winter) may leave them without whatever food they have "squirreled" away.

Squirrels, of course, are not the issue. My consciousness is. I'm making decisions from my ego, not my heart. My ego says squirrels are worthy of my anxiety. My heart says, "Silly boy." What happens to the squirrels, or to my office, or to terrorists, or to the starving millions, or to my own body—is never the real question. Me living in my heart is. How do I shift? By feeling the fear that drives this "reasoning" and letting it go. It's just energy. On my better days I salute the descendants of Bullwinkle's sidekick munching birdseed outside my office window. Everyone is our teacher.

I'm not convinced that becoming enlightened means changing myself. Change, it seems to me, can imply a certain violence, a certain judgment that there's something "wrong," that we are somehow deficient, inadequate, flawed. Perhaps the only thing that needs to change is that opinion. Right and wrong don't exist in any ultimate vibration of Spirit that I've ever experienced. Only our ego plays the blame game. Only our ego "condemns." Only our ego needs to "fix" things. The guidance I receive is that surrender to Spirit means loving myself as I am, listening to my heart, and following directions.

Which is where living in heaven and complaining comes in.

My pop used to say that there are some people who, if you gave them a wheelbarrow full of gold bars, would kick about the terrible burden they had to heft. That's me. I ask God to live in me consciously so that I can feel His presence. God says fine. First, He gives me astonishing teachers, a spiritual family that is about as close to unprecedented as you can imagine, and a number of beautiful friends. Even my birth family are people with big hearts. He introduces me to spiritual practices which deepen my attunement and hasten my unfolding. I live in one of the most physically serene places on earth. I have more freedom in how I use my time than almost anyone I know. Cancer notwithstanding, my body works well. Without trying terribly hard I've always had a little money. I graduated next-to-last in my high school class, yet was given a free ride to one of the most selective colleges in America, Amherst, from which I graduated with honors. All this immeasurable support and inspiration is God's perversity. "In this life, buddy boy," He says, "you will have everything a person could want. So anytime you start whining, remember: It's all about you, and your unwillingness to love yourself."

Knowing that, I still find plenty to fuss about—preferring to hold on to the familiar of fear rather than leap into the void of love. So-and-so isn't doing what I feel s/he should. This corner of the universe could do with a touch of tidying. I wish I were this or that. Not to mention the ever-deadly "If only…"

How does God respond to my complaining? He says fine. He is always willing to offer the next level of support, if that's what we need, to help us wise up to what's essential and what's not. It is in this context that I have met my latest teacher, cancer: here to stay for what looks like the duration. After about a week of quietly getting acquainted, I realized that I was more present than ever before, and profoundly less afraid. By "present" I mean having my consciousness in my body and breath, grounded in the earth, rather than dissipated with thoughts of the past or future.

For more than thirty years I've been inspired by the sentiment of a desert monk from the first century A.D., who wrote that the person who keeps death before his eyes will always overcome his cowardice. Experiencing the reality of that promise has been among my ongoing practices, and now the opportunity is richer than ever. I am grateful to whoever it was who said nothing focuses the mind quite like knowing you're going to be hanged in the morning. The humor in that remark is its truth. And its truth to me, I'm finding, is an amazing blessing.

At the same time, there is a particular quality of pain that cancer illuminates. It is beyond the pain of those who love me as they respond to the prospect of my physical demise. The pain I'm talking about is the pain of missed opportunity; the pain of the harm we create any time we deny the sacredness of the moment we're in (any time we are not present, choosing not to connect our mind and heart); and the pain of needing this exquisite teacher, this gift, because my actions have not kept pace with my desire for Oneness.

But the lesson is not to beat myself up for who I haven't been. Rather, it is to forgive myself: to feel the pain of choices made in fear and, like everything else, surrender it to the One. The more I do that, the more I feel the Divine dancing under my skin. For that awakening, I can only bow in gratitude.

Spring Shows Us Our True Selves

*Spring is when we might see
a young boy and girl, each with chartreuse hair,
standing together on the bare back of an
emerald horse trotting through a pasture
sprinkled with dandelions.*

O N APRIL 12, 1934 the wind atop Mt. Washington in New Hampshire reached 231 miles an hour. It was probably a good thing I wasn't born yet because when I was a teenager (a condition that lasted until I was 45) my motto was "Nothing is too intense for me." God's primary job, so far as I can tell, is responding to silly categorical statements like that—by introducing us to circumstances that suggest perhaps we're not quite the smarty pants we thought we were. Today, I have an indelible awareness of what frightens me to the core, and seldom is it more alive than during the season of Spring. I can be uncomfortable around daffodils.

When Nelson Mandela became President of South Africa, his inaugural address included a poem that begins: *Our greatest fear is not that we are inadequate, but that we are powerful beyond measure.*

This is among the messages of Spring, that splendiferous celebration of the unconditional nurturing, compassion and pizzazz that is the Earth Mother, the mother of us all.

When else but Spring could the color green have been invented? Every shade of viridescence imaginable leaps out of the closet, ready for anything. Every tree is dressed to kill. Every bush shimmies like a sequined gown on a belly dancer. Every lawn lusts for the caress of bare feet, the cut of a sharp blade, and the kiss of dog poop. And near sunset, when the light is just so, Spring is when we

might see a young boy and girl, each with chartreuse hair, standing together on the bare back
of an emerald horse trotting through a pasture
sprinkled with dandelions.

Spring is a golf course that forbids tradi-
tional golf attire and instead provides players
access to every sort of clown costuming the
world has ever known—including wigs and
hats and jackets and tights, noses and knickers
and stupendous bow-ties (and of course all col-
or of shoes, each the size of a watermelon)—
from which guests create the ensemble of their
choice for the day's round.

Spring is the trio of Elvis, Beethoven and
Ella Fitzgerald knocking out gospel tunes for
the *Heaven Ain't For Weenies* label.

No wonder Spring is dangerous! It shows
us our true self, the part of us passionate to live
in the vibration of joy.

That's bad enough. But implicit in that
revelation is the request to give up whatever is
in the way of actually embracing the "real" us.
Which means we are being asked to be willing—that's all, just willing—to engage in that

lifelong practice of surrendering our attachments to smallness. Oh, I'm so unworthy or un-something, we cry. Nonsense, says Spring in the voice of the Mormon Tabernacle Choir. You are powerful beyond measure.

Reminders like that can be a bit unsettling if, like me, you've spent a lot of time running away from the magnificence of the true you.

My understanding of what a fugitive I can be surfaced in a very ordinary way. I was an active alcoholic and dope smoker for many years before bottoming out two decades ago and choosing to live sober. I'm always happy to identify myself as an alcoholic or drug addict, but one of the many things I've learned during sobriety is that my addiction goes far beyond chemical intoxicants. My addiction is to anything that keeps me from me. It can be work, play, anger, blame, worthy causes—and in my case, building large stone sculptures on my farm, which I've been doing with gusto for the past few years. Heck, I can use hiking a mountain or watching a cloud to keep me from being present in the here and now.

What am I afraid of? The absolute, immeasurable, unending, limitless, unbounded, inexhaustible and otherwise pretty darn big Love that is the essential "stuff" of the universe—the essential "stuff" of us all.

In other words, I'm afraid of myself. And because Spring reminds me who I really am, those pesky daffodils can set my heart atremble.

I Am a Terrorist

*Perhaps the greatest power we humans enjoy is
the power of choice.*

I AM A TERRORIST, and proud of it. Does
that rile you—that I have the brass to make
such an incendiary claim? I pray that it does.
For it means that you are my puppet. I quack
and you twitch.

I hope you find this offensive, because
then I will have demonstrated just how easy it
is for me to undermine your belief that you are
an independent thinker.

And if now you're thinking, "This fool's
making me mad," guess what? In fewer than

100 words, you have relinquished to me your most precious possession: responsibility for your peace of mind.

Is anything more foolish?

Please pardon my tabloid attempt to get a rise out of you. I would never intentionally do harm. Yet I'm happy to go to the Policeman's Ball dressed as Osama bin Laden if it helps us be more aware of how we allow external circumstances to hijack our well-being—and how unhealthy that is. When they publish a list of the biggest myths of all time, those in the family of "So-and-so made me angry" will be right up there with "The earth is flat" and "My hamster was Elvis in a previous life."

I'm not denying the vast pain throughout the world. I'm questioning that it need define us. The gift of terrorism is its reminder that "security" can be found only in our own heart.

Consider this: Perhaps the greatest power we humans enjoy is the power of choice. And perhaps our gravest shortcoming is that we forget that we possess this power. Not that we're completely free to choose whether we become the first stuttering anchor with purple hair on the network evening news. But in every moment we make a much more important choice: whether to cherish our peace of mind or give it away.

Among the most painful telephone calls I've received from my son in prison was the one that began with me saying, "What's happening?" and him replying, "Nothing's happening, Dad. Whadaya think? I'm in prison." It was painful because, in that moment, my boy was choosing to have his sense of possibility dictated by something outside himself. And it was painful because of how often I make the same choice.

Recently I heard a guy on a TV commercial say, "The one thing I hate is dandelions."

Boy, I would love to be him.

If the one thing I hated was dandelions, that would mean I had moved beyond stuff like child abusers, the fact that a third of the world goes to bed hungry every night, and (too often tops on my list) whiners, name-callers and other sniveling noodle-spines who blame others for their misery. If I've said it once I've said it 100 times: If it weren't for them, I'd be happy.

I once got a rooster as a birthday present from a dear friend. Not the walking, talking, cock-a-doodle-do type of rooster, but the kind Tiffany's might sell. In this case, gold and porcelain and small enough to rest on a slice of Wonder Bread. It was my friend's way of reminding me that anger is a precious gift because it is the rooster of spiritual awakening, alerting us to the fear that is crowing for our attention, calling to be set free.

That rooster hangs in the window overlooking my desk. Sometimes I duct-tape it to my forehead.

I've made up a spiritual law. It's called Divine Perversity. Divine Perversity is when the universe asks us to teach that which we most have to learn. An egomaniac extolling the virtues of humility—that sort of thing. With me, it's that everything is a gift. My job description is celebrating that principle.

"Everything is a gift" is both the most inspiring and terrifying of possibilities. Every familiar disappears when we stop passing judgment and instead open ourselves to how and why the present moment is here solely to help us grow our compassion, understanding and what Albert Schweitzer called our reverence for life.

Someone once said to me, "If I give up blame, what the heck am I going to talk about?"

I told you I was a terrorist. Or at least I'm trying to be. The Terrorist of Love. Dangerous, but not harmful.

THE COURAGE TO CELEBRATE

*I have a poster more valuable than the Mona Lisa,
and I'd be happy to give it to you.*

O N AT LEAST A HALF-DOZEN occasions
over the past 30 years, one or more emi-
nent physicians has said that, very likely, my
daughter Kathryn was going to die soon. It
started when she was nine and diagnosed with
a form of bone cancer that had killed virtually
every child in its path before it got to her.

Kathryn's options were either certain
death or an experimental treatment which included amputating one of her legs and under-

going a regimen of painful chemotherapy that also might kill her.

She recently turned 40. Along the way from then to now have been a number of other nearly fatal events, all of them related to the original cancer and its treatment.

Today, professionally, Kathryn is considered one of the bright lights of her generation. The particulars don't matter for the purposes of this tale except to say that, as a visible and respected person, she is often told how courageous she is for having overcome so much adversity.

She says baloney.

"If God gave me the chance to live my life over without cancer and heart failure and being an amputee and all the rest, I wouldn't take it. Better hair, maybe. The rest, fuhgedaboutit."

I once heard a war correspondent remark that when the bullets first start flying in your direction, one of two things happens: You become a blob of pudding, or you develop a wicked sense of humor.

Kathryn might take that one step further and say there's also the choice to see the gift that accompanies those bullets—a teacher helping to bring forward parts of us we never knew were there.

Which reminds me, I have a poster more valuable than the Mona Lisa, and I'd be happy to give it to you. No joke.

The image on my poster, created by one of the delightful illustrators of our day, Jeff Moores, is of Noah waterskiing behind the ark. The man is most decidedly having a good time. It may be pouring rain, not a speck of land in sight, but Noah isn't fazed. He's having a ball. As are all the animals on board cheering his performance.

Under the image is the headline: *Being Alive is Knowing How to Celebrate.*

Why do I feel my poster is more valuable than DaVinci's masterpiece (besides the possibility that I'm a nutcase)? Because it encourages us to ask ourselves: "What will it take for me to celebrate in the face of adversity?" That question contains a key to happiness. And, like all such questions, answering it requires courage.

That's because celebration—as I find it anyway—is so much more than a party, or a wing-ding to note an achievement. Celebration is not something we *earn*—like dessert after eating our peas. Celebration is actually the very essence of life. It's what we must do all the time to have the life we want.

Which is why true celebration can be as scary as it is rewarding, for it is the practice of honoring the sacredness of *everything* that has brought us to this moment—every experience we've ever had, frankly—then giving it away, freeing ourselves of it so that we may step into the present completely open to all that the present has to offer.

If all the holy books ever written were distilled to a half-dozen bumper stickers, *Be Here Now* would doubtless be one of them. Isn't that what we're all trying to accomplish: to be as fully present as possible?

How do we do that without bowing with reverence to every single part of us?

At the same time, how do we do it if we're carrying around the past like a backpack full of bowling balls? Or if our attention is perpetually around the next corner lest a fire-breathing Chihuahua be lurking there?

There are many reasons my daughter isn't dead yet. Three of them are medical wizardry, a wicked sense of humor, and the fact that you can celebrate just fine no matter how many legs you have.

P.S. Information on ordering a Noah poster can be found on my website:
CoolMindWarmHeart.com
(Look under "Noah.")

THE ELUSIVE MEANING OF "SUPPORT OUR TROOPS"

Imagine if "Support Our Troops" were the banner for a national dialogue where each of us was encouraged to explore and discuss what the phrase meant to us.

T HE MAN WHO OWNS the garage where my car is doctored is the father of a soldier who recently returned from a tour in Iraq. "Now the healing begins," the father told me.

This father has held his breath for a year, aware that every ring of the phone (and his garage is popular, so the phone rings often) might be the call that will rip his heart out. And now, even with his son on American soil (temporarily, anyway), the dad continues to hold his breath, given the internal challenges his boy is likely to face. It's no secret that the suicide rate among combat soldiers in Iraq is disturbingly high. Whatever the reasons for that statistic, I'm sure they contribute to complicating many a returning soldier's reentry to so-called "normal life."

The story of this dad and his son couldn't be more commonplace (although it certainly doesn't feel that way to those involved): soldiers in war zones living amidst the kind of insanity that eats the soul, while their loved ones are given lessons in helplessness that they had hoped they might never experience.

Against this backdrop of national heartache stands a symbol that, to me, exacerbates as much as it may heal the wounds of war. I'm speaking of the slogan "Support Our Troops."

Years ago in an Oklahoma airport near Fort Sill, I noticed a young man wearing a baseball cap with the phrase "Nuke 'em till they glow" printed where the team logo usually rides. Without getting into the merits of the sentiment, I think its meaning is pretty clear.

Sadly, the same cannot be said about "Support Our Troops."

Beyond being a call to action that hardly anyone could argue with (alongside "Support Our Children" and "Support Our Schools"), "Support Our Troops" is a phrase so empty of explicit meaning that it cannot represent a clear, collective commitment. If we delve an inch under the surface, does the "Support Our Troops" decal on your car mean the same as the one on mine? I wouldn't bet a day's pay that it does. To some, supporting our troops means approving the use of American military force to further democracy around the world. To others, supporting our troops means bringing them home from this present engagement in Iraq while they're still alive—as in, immediately. And to be sure, there are a host of other possible interpretations in between, including a simple non-political offering of love.

In some previous life (or two or three), I must have been viciously manipulative because in this life I find that quality hard to indulge. One reason "Support Our Troops" is painful is that I have yet to make peace with the part of me that could have dreamed it up: the part willing to shape-shift reality into whatever form will meet my ends. (If you were hired on New Year's Eve and fired on New Year's Day, why can't your resume say you were on the job two years?)

Because its potential inferences are endless, "Support Our Troops" exudes that energy of manipulation, that attempt at seduction. It's as though the brain trust that created it was charged with developing a statement related to the Iraq invasion that the fewest number of Americans could take exception to—thereby enlisting the tacit (and unwitting) endorsement by many citizens of the government's choice to wage this particular war. Despite its considerable human misery, I find the war less destructive to our nation's well-being than this snake-oil attempt to have me support it.

Feel the thread of anger in those last two paragraphs. It would be a mistake for me, or you, to think that what I am really writing about is something going on "out there" in society, separate from myself. That is never the case. In fact, anytime we are angry about any so-called "external" event, our anger is really a signal, a wake-up call, that there is something about ourselves we have yet to love. No one has ever made me, or you, angry—or happy for that matter. Our every response to life is a choice. External events have only one purpose, and that is to show us ourselves: to show us where our attention will most serve our primary aspiration as evolving spiritual beings—to grow our capacity to love. And we grow our love by the continual practice of letting go of fear (anger being one of fear's many faces, as is unforgiveness, guilt and shame). So the gift of this essay for me is that it calls me to act—to love myself by forgiving the part of me who, holding onto fear, has blown smoke at others in order to get his own way. Everything is 100 percent about us. And part of us is America.

History suggests that one essential quality for the long-term health of an institution is clarity of values and purpose. For sustained vitality, it matters less what the specific values are, or what the purpose is, than it does having clarity on them. "Support Our Troops" does not meet this test of clarity and therefore is symptomatic of an institution—a nation—severely challenged to sustain itself with dignity.

Imagine if "Support Our Troops" were the banner for a national dialogue where each of us was encouraged to explore and discuss what the phrase meant to us. Sure, it would trigger some intense debate, but since when does keeping ourselves closed to the views of others grow understanding? The strength of America is its diversity. The Achilles heel of America is the inability to make room for differences. If there is a single reason why our nation is becoming an increasingly polarized culture it is that we don't talk with one another enough. We don't ask the simplest of questions: What does this mean to you? Imagine spending as much time focused on what unites us as we do on what separates us. Feel for a moment the fear at all levels of our society, including within yourself, that inhibits such talking—and listening. And wherever there is fear, there is harm to the human family.

If "Support Our Troops" were the catalyst for conversation, I believe that our collective sense of values and purpose would become clearer in at least one important way: our common desire that every American soldier be given the best opportunity to survive his or her military service with the rest of their life full of possibility before them.

And if that's what we wish for our soldiers, why wouldn't we wish the same for the soldiers of any nation—even those we feel obliged to kill? Maybe someday the sign will read "Support All Troops."

A Great Way to Die

Isn't it beautiful how seven astronauts
(about whom I know nothing except how they died)
can shine new light on my heart's passion,
and how I often run from it.

T HE SPACE SHUTTLE Columbia had ex-
ploded in flight. All seven astronauts
were presumed dead. The NPR commentators
characterized the event as *tragic, a disaster, a terrible accident*, and so forth. Who could argue?
Yet, there I was, slamming the steering wheel
with the heel of my hand, saying: "Man, what
a great way to die."

Listening to the story unfold, I had imagined myself before the Columbia mission ask-

ing each of the crew how he or she would choose to exit this life if given a say in the matter. And I imagined each replying, "Easy. Doing what I love most: being an astronaut."

That answer came to haunt me.

What would it take for me to say the same, I wondered—that I died doing what I loved most? And more to the point, why didn't I have an answer? How come I had never considered how I would like to leave this life? Why had I avoided envisioning such a basic, and inevitable, event?

A study at Ford Motor Company is revealing. Many of us make a big deal of planning, goal setting, management by objective and all, yet fewer than five percent of us (based on research among Ford employees) have substantial long-term goals that we actually write down. The irony, the Ford findings suggest, is that people who have substantial goals *and* write them down are 85 percent more successful (i.e., having the life they want, rather than the life they're stuck with) than the rest of us.

So the question is: Why *don't* we create a vision of our future, and when we do, why don't we write it down?

There may be many answers, but the one I'm most familiar with is this: We are afraid of committing to what we actually want because we feel we don't deserve to have it. And/or, we don't want to feel the pain of not achieving our desire, which really means we don't want to feel the pain of the ways in which we sabotage our dreams.

I was in my 50s before I finally made writing more than a way to make a living. The pain of not following my heart finally surpassed the fear of confronting my own shallowness. That, and feeling unworthy of the joy that comes from jumping into the complete unknown— every day—just to find out what the heck's going on in there.

An avatar friend of mine says that every circumstance can be managed in a healthy manner by the judicious use of a single question: Who am I? It took many years for me to be willing to follow that question wherever it led. Which isn't to say I'm good at it. Just willing. I feel a little like a spelunker, an explorer of underground caves, and writing is the light on my safety helmet illuminating the darkness a few feet in front of wherever I point my head.

The reason I've avoided how I would like to die, I realize as I am writing this, is that it brings me face to face with how much I dance around what I want most in life. Ironic, isn't it? To be passionate for something and yet afraid of what it asks. I don't want to "be" anything- not even kind, compassionate, intelligent, responsible, productive, or useful. I just want to love. The rest, I'm confident, will take care of itself. And since love, whatever else it may be, is the practice of letting go of fear, I figure I've got plenty to keep me out of mischief for the rest of this incarnation anyway.

Robin Williams says death is nature's way of saying, Your table's ready. So here I am, loosening the fear of commitment, listening to the whisper within, and now, finally, ready to write down what I'd like to be doing when the Maitre d' appears.

And wouldn't you know. It doesn't matter. What I'm doing when I die. On the outside, I mean. There are so many things I love. But they are just preferences. Even things I might not choose on any conscious level, such as leaving at the end of a long illness, are beside the point.

Gandhi had the right idea. His intention, which he achieved even while being killed by an assassin's bullet, was to leave this life with the name of God on his lips. Rather the ultimate in "long-term goals," wouldn't you say? But not the easiest of deaths to pull off, since it demands that we are ever fully present moment by moment, surrendering every fear, every desire, every expectation, every addiction, every attachment to past and future, again and again—and that God lives in our mouth, inspiring every word we speak, so that His name is literally on the tip of our tongue all the time.

Yet that's the death I want, now that I'm finally getting around to saying so. Whether I slip on a banana peel at the edge of the Grand Canyon or get eaten by a boa constrictor (*Wha-*

daya know, it's nibblin' my toe. Oh gee, it's up to my knee...) I'll be doing what I love most: becoming who I truly am. Who all of us are, really.

The universe is sneaky. I can't have the death I want without having the life I want.

Isn't it beautiful how seven astronauts (about whom I know nothing except how they died) can shine new light on my heart's passion, and how I often run from it.

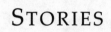

STORIES

PREMUMBLE

SOMETIMES WHEN PEOPLE read the stories that follow, they say, "One minute I think this is all made up, the next I'm sure it's a memoir or an essay of some sort. How much of it is real?"

I smile because I have the same problem.

Here's where I come out. Our life is a practice of learning to live from our heart, that part of us at One with all of existence. These stories convey as truthfully as I know how (which is not necessarily saying much) the experience of my heart. *Shiny Balls of Light*, the first story, does revolve around one certifiable historical figure, Paramahansa Yogananda, who died more than 50 years ago. No, he and I never met in the flesh, nor do I speak for any organization created in his name. But like everything else in life, since energy doesn't lie, your own heart will tell you what's real and what isn't.

Shiny Balls of Light

1

The Abduction

WHEN I WAS FOUR, my mother and father took me with them to this gigantic event in New York City's Central Park: a Tibetan celebration from sunrise to sunset on the day of maximum light—Summer solstice—a day beautiful in every way imaginable until I was abducted. Since our home was a ranch east of Los Angeles, our nearest neighbor the better part of a mile away, the gathering was the first time that I experienced so many people so close. It was unbelievably thrilling. But most thrilling of all was seeing so many famil-

iar faces. Well, not faces exactly; familiar beings more like. One woman, who easily might
have been mistaken for a child playing dress-
up, was seated on a nearby blanket with some
friends, all of whom were probably college stu-
dents. Her face's youth was belied by a de-
meanor that, I've learned since, held the kind
of fearless patience that comes to some people
who are intimate with terminal illness. Unlike
her friends, this woman knew she wasn't inde-
structible. (Lady Death is the name I've given
her.) Whatever illness it was, an ebony cane lay
at her side and, looking through her skin (one
of the talents I had as a youngster that went the
way of milk teeth), I could see her heart pump-
ing much faster than my own. I recalled that
she had loved strawberries. So I took a straw-
berry from the picnic the hotel had packed for
us, walked over and offered it to her. I was surprised she didn't remember me. We had
known each other as children, boys, in a former
life where we had eaten a pile of strawberries
together by a stream and then jumped naked
into the water. It had been one of those unfor-

gettable moments in that life. I don't know where this was, but our skin was rather dark. In Central Park that day, I was still learning that not everyone has glimpses of their previous incarnations. Not everyone senses how connected we all are.

It's not that I remembered everything about a person (nor do I today). Usually, it was just a flash of a moment we had shared, like the strawberries.

Lady Death said to me, "Ooooh, aren't you sweet? Thank you." To her friends, she said, "My favorite fruit in all the world." (Cravings carry over from one life to the next, the Swami once told me. If we die with the jones for curry, we may find ourselves reborn in India.)

Throughout the day, Lady Death looked at me from time to time, and I could tell she felt something, but didn't know what it was. There were no flashes at all for her. As I say, I came to understand that that's how most people respond to the world around them. They occasionally have some vague sense of connection, but for all sorts of reasons don't honor it, don't open to it, don't feel that it means enough to pursue.

The heat of the day had begun to wane and I was standing on the grass a few feet from my parents. They were lying on the gold blanket they'd borrowed from the hotel, eyes closed, listening to the Tibetan Tantric Choir perform live their "throat singing" amplified through huge speakers so that a hundred thousand people could hear them. My mother's head rested on my dad's slim belly, her auburn curls offset by his blue checked shirt with the pearl buttons. I have no photos to prove it, but it's a safe bet I was wearing jeans, t-shirt and cowboy boots. I was trying to get the hang of that rubber ball tied to a paddle with a rubber string thing when suddenly I'm lifted up from behind and carried away by a woman, not so tall but very strong, who smelled worse than a dead deer with its back end ripped open by coyotes, to that point in my life the most revolting odor I'd encountered.

I had never really been afraid before, surprising as that sounds. It wasn't the fear of some external danger exactly, as much as it was the fear of being separated from my parents, an event without precedent. If I'm not mistaken I'd never had a babysitter.

Yet, I was too shocked to cry out, and in the woman's grip I was essentially paralyzed. She held me so tight that, to this day, I have a star-shaped scar at the base of my skull. My head must have pressed against a metal button or pin she was wearing. It looks like I've been branded on my medulla, the principle point where life force enters the body.

The woman, her putrid breath slow and steady as a respirator, walked fast with me for what seemed a long while, then, without stopping, put me down—and before I thought to turn and look, disappeared into the crowd. She never said a word. I never actually saw her. All I remember of her is her smell, which I would recognize even today, more than 70 years later. I did eventually learn who she was, but that's not relevant here.

I was alone for the first time. Not alone the way most people think of it. Rather, it was the kind of alone I've since experienced in the hearts of some children who never meet their biological mother. Or whose father is jealous of them from birth. Or whose parents have no familiarity with the geography of emotions. It is an emptiness that is, to this day, impossible to put into words.

I have no memory of crying, but I'm sure I must have. No one came to my aid in any event. In fact, all I do remember about those first moments alone pales in significance to my one feeling. Terror. There was not a person I recognized. There was no one whose skin I could see under. I felt no connection of inner hearts. It was as though I had been taken to another world. And although the people looked like me in a general sense, in reality they were all strangers. I didn't know it at the time, but I was seeing the world as most people do.

I've walked the 800-plus acres of Central Park a few times as an adult, and my best guess is that I must have been at least a half-mile from my parents, which of course, for a four-year-old, is Mars.

I sat under a tree. Waiting to be found, I suppose.

After a while, I got up and started to walk. I had no plan, no destination. I was four. I just walked. And as I walked, I started to hear what I call my guides talking to me.

Guides have been part of my life since birth, but at first they didn't say anything. They were just there, loving me. Everyone has them. I just happened to feel mine. The very first actual message (that I remember) came one morning when I was still in a high chair. The message was that this life was a dream, and that when it was over I would awaken where guides would be all I saw. At the time, the message had no real impact on me; it was just a message. After that, until that day in Central Park, I received messages only when I would ask a question. (I once asked why my best friend Freddy Kleehammer's spirit woke me up one night, and I was told that he was leaving his body. Freddy's spirit had been crying. Next morning my mother told me that Freddy and his mom had been killed when a train hit their car at a railroad crossing. This was about six months before my Central Park experience. Years later, my guides showed me that Freddy's mom had planned their meeting with the train.) The point here is, if I didn't ask a question, and I seldom did, my guides didn't "speak." They were just there.

However, walking in Central Park that day, with what seemed to be the entire population of the world around me, my guides started actively directing me.

The first message was to follow the fat woman in the black dress who was walking next to the lake. I ended up following her to a large round pond. In the middle of the pond was a tall fountain with an angel on top. I gawked at the angel so long that when I finally looked around, Black Dress Woman was gone. But then I was told to follow a shirtless man covered in tattoos and carrying an infant in a sling across his chest. When Tattoo Man stopped for an ice cream, I was told to stand

144

next to the ice cream man. All in white—pants, shirt and baseball cap—Ice Cream Man, a crowd around him, seemed to make his treats appear from out of nowhere, like a magician, presenting them to his customers as if he were offering them gold. He spoke in a Spanish accent that was probably Puerto Rican, though I didn't know it at the time. All I knew was that he wasn't Mexican, the only Spanish I was familiar with. His "store" was a white pickup truck with white tires. In the truck's bed was a large white freezer with four small doors on the back side. Painted on the side of the freezer was the picture of a lion swinging on a swing while licking an ice cream cone. I stood next to Ice Cream Man for quite a while until he noticed me.

"Ah, Marco Polo," he said, whereupon he opened one of his freezer doors and brought out an orange Popsicle, my favorite, presenting it to me with considerable flourish. He never asked for money.

"Ahora, busca tu mama," he said, patting my head.

To many, this story sounds fantastic, which is why, unless I'm guided to, I don't share much of my inner life. It asks too much of most people. I get into enough trouble as is.

It wasn't like there was a running commentary in my head—there were no words. It was more like I was being physically guided. As I walked by a man on a bench, he called, "Hey sonny," and all of a sudden I started to run as if I were being pushed from behind by a giant hand.

One of the Tibetan lamas was sitting on a platform under a big red and gold canopy talking to lots and lots of people who were seated on the grass in front of him. With his maroon robes and shaved head, he was different from anyone I had ever seen, yet somehow he was familiar. He had the kindest, gentlest smile, crooked teeth and very big ears. I was told to go up and sit on his lap. The audience may have been surprised, but he didn't seem to be. In fact, it was funny. He put our foreheads together, and I heard him speak, not from his mouth, but right from his head into mine.

"Hello, brother. It's good to see you again." He gave me a piece of crystallized ginger candy. Then he stood me up and patted me on the fanny and I ran out of the tent hearing his laugh and the laughter of the audience behind me.

A hand caught my arm. A blonde teenage girl in a blue dress with yellow stars asked if I knew where my parents were. I was told to point in a certain direction. She said, "Hop in," nodding to a kid's red wagon she was pulling. As we went along, she kept turning to me. "Now where?" and I kept pointing where I was told to.

I wish I could say that my parents were still napping when I returned, and that I realized that virtually no time had passed from when Dead Deer Woman took me to when Wagon Girl brought me back. That sort of stuff would happen later in life. The truth itself, however, was pretty amazing. My father, the famous horse whisperer, taught both children of New York City's Police Commissioner. His kids came to our ranch for a couple of weeks in the summer. My dad had all the Commissioner's personal phone numbers. Every cop in the city had a description of me and Dead Deer Woman. Roadblocks had been set up. K-9 teams had sniffed the jacket I'd worn that morning and were in pursuit. The miracle was that I had made it back to my mother's arms before anybody spotted me. She was alone, sitting on the gold blanket, my dad out searching.

Mother screamed my name.

I threw myself at her and held on with every ounce of strength I had. We rolled around on the blanket, she patting me all over, kissing me, laughing, crying. At that point in my life, my mother was still breast feeding me on occasion, and now that I had her arms around me, her milk was what I craved more than anything in the world.

"Where did you find him?" Mom said to Wagon Girl, holding me in her lap, combing my hair with her fingers, occasional tears dropping onto my face as I nursed.

"Way up on the other end of the park," Wagon Girl said. "I asked him if he knew where his parents were, and I just followed wherever he pointed. It's obvious he comes here a lot. He knew exactly how to find you."

When I was older my mother told me, "At that moment I realized that I was simply your babysitter. Your real mom was the mother of us all."

Even at four, I knew that that day was the start of my life in the world: listening and following.

2

The Swami

I HAD JUST TURNED EIGHT when I met the
Swami. For some reason the very first question I asked him was "How old are you?" He
laughed and said, "You are asking the age of
my house. My house is fifty-seven. But a
house is nothing. What's important is the soul
who lives there. And my soul is the same as
yours. Ageless."

I had no idea what he meant.

Our ranch was near the Mojave Desert,
east of Los Angeles. Turning eight, I was per-

mitted to ride Lady, my Palomino, anywhere I wanted so long as I could still see our property, and the Swami's place, a mile away, was the furthest point I could go and still make out the stand of willows overlooking our pond. He was our closest neighbor, although he was seldom there.

"Feel free to get acquainted," my mom said. "I hear he's a very nice man."

The first time I rode to the Swami's, no one was home. The second time, he was outside with a couple of men who were building a stone wall around a garden. I later found out that these workmen were monks who had joined the religious community the Swami had started many years earlier when he arrived in the U.S. from India. I also came to learn that the Swami's fellowship had a big headquarters in L.A., a number of churches and other sorts of places, but that this particular spot was used as the Swami's personal retreat. Very few people were ever there with the Swami, just a handful of the monks and occasionally a couple of the sisters, or nuns.

On the day I rode up, the Swami was watching one of the monks attempt to put a rattlesnake over the stone wall so that the rattler would be in the desert, not in the garden they were trying to enclose. I reined Lady, without saying a word, curled one leg around the saddle horn and sat looking down from her as the workman tried unsuccessfully several times to lift the curled snake with a long-handled shovel. I could tell the man was petrified, and the snake wasn't too pleased either.

I was what you might call a snake charmer. I don't know why, but I was born with an understanding of snakes. It was like I could read their minds. Really, I think it was that snakes could read my mind. They knew I wasn't a predator. I'd picked up many a rattler and played with it. So when I saw this workman afraid, as most people are, my first instinct was to help. I was just about to say, "Mister, I can get that snake over for you," when the Swami looked up at me, smiled, and give his head a little shake "No." The Swami had read my mind. No one had ever done that before. Just as surprising to me, I knew for certain that the Swami was also a snake charmer. He could have picked up the snake himself and not thought twice about it. He was the only other snake charmer I had ever met, and he was even better than I was because he could have communicated with that snake by some sort of mental telepathy and had the snake leave the garden of its own accord. But, I somehow got, the Swami was teaching the man to have faith in the Swami's power to protect him. It was obvious that the man needed the Swami's protection, since the man was a long way from understanding the snake. I felt the Swami ask the snake to cooperate. The snake stretched out, a very un-snake-like thing to do when there's a man with a shovel and the man is afraid. The monk grabbed the snake's tail and whipped the rattler into the air and away from the garden as quickly as he could. Unfortunately for the monk, he didn't aim, and the snake sailed right at me and wrapped around my neck. All I could do was sit quietly and let the snake regain its equilibrium. Had Lady been almost any other horse, she would have bolted. Most horses hate snakes. But Lady had been trained by my dad, which is a whole other story. The monk was sure he'd killed me. Finally, I took off my hat and turned it upside down in my lap so the snake could slide down my chest and cozy himself inside the hat if he wished, which he did. I then dismounted and put my hat on the ground, and shortly the snake had had enough excitement for one day and slithered off for parts unknown. The monk looked like he'd seen a miracle, which, on his terms, I suppose he had. The Swami said to the men, 'Why don't you boys get back to work now,' and then gestured for me to join him on the veranda.

"So," the Swami said, once I had hitched Lady and accepted the glass of lemonade he offered, " we meet again."

The greeting didn't surprise me. No flashes told me when or how, but my heart knew that the Swami and I had met before. But one thing did scare the heck out of me. And that was how deeply I felt that the Swami knew and

loved me more than any other person on earth
· ever would.

Thus began the most important two and a
half years of my life.

He wasn't a very tall man, the Swami, not
much taller than that long-handled shovel the
monk couldn't quite get to work. And he was
plump, there's just no other word for it. By
plump, I by no means imply that he was in the
slightest unhealthy, lethargic, slow, or even old,
for he was just as much the opposite of all those
qualities as I was. I've always had the impres-
sion that he had to be a little roly-poly in order
to carry around all the energy inside him; he
would have burned up a skinny body. His hair
was long, beyond his shoulders, slightly curly,
and black without ever having known a strand
of gray, I would bet. His skin was a color so
much its own that it is impossible for me to put
a single word on it. What I remember is the vi-
sual combination of milk chocolate and rose lit
from beneath by a light so golden and bright
that, if you were to cut the Swami with a knife,
instead of drawing blood, you would reveal

the sun. The skin of his face was soft; his beard almost non-existent; I'm sure he shaved every day, but not because his entire face required it. His face made me smile. There was always kindness in his expression, even when he would tell me stories of people betraying him, such as the man he loved very much who had stolen a large amount of money from him, or another man who had poisoned the Swami's dog. His eyes, however, could stop a train. They saw everything. It's hard to explain. When he looked at you, you knew he saw everything about you, and he loved every single bit of it, even the parts he suggested (and sometimes more than suggested) that you change. But then, when you looked into his eyes you also saw that his consciousness, while paying attention to you, also was elsewhere. Well, not just elsewhere: attuned to the entire universe. I came to discover that two or more people in completely different locations might report that they had seen him, in the flesh, and even talked with him, at exactly the same time.

Why the first words out of my mouth were 'How old are you?' I may never know. Perhaps it was just one of those questions that helps to reestablish a sense of reality with somebody you know you know but can't quite remember. I was eight years old. I didn't live in the world of religious beliefs. We didn't go to church, didn't belong to any denomination. In my family, everything was sacred, even if we didn't understand it. When your life is horses and the desert, that's not a surprising view. What you don't respect can kill you. I did know that I felt the world in ways that many other people did not. And with the Swami that afternoon, I felt so much love pouring into me that I wondered whether I was about to turn into that shiny ball of light that my dad was always saying we all were. Which may be why my second question to the Swami was, "Are you God?"

He chuckled. "No more than you."

He wasn't God, but in years to come I would understand that his consciousness and God's consciousness were one. He explained to me that he had been my guru for several lives. One reason he used this retreat, he said, was so that we would have the opportunity to meet again.

"It's not just in previous lives that we've known each other, you know," the Swami said one day. "Remember the woman who abducted you in Central Park?" He smiled at the surprise on my face. I hadn't yet told him that story. "What is it you call her, Dead Deer Woman?" he said. "Well, that was me. Awakening you to the call of your heart."

"Well, I'm glad you smell different today," I said.

He patted my arm. "I had to completely mask my identity to distract you from feeling the depth of my love for you."

"What about the star scar?"

"A kiss."

The Swami spent most of his days at the retreat either in solitude or writing. And yet he invited me to be with him whenever I could, which was quite extraordinary, considering that even the location of the retreat was kept secret from all but his closest disciples. Several days could pass without the phone ringing. His writing often meant dictating to a secretary or to a team of secretaries working in tandem, because he could speak for hours without interruption, stopping only for a sip of water. Yet, when I would arrive and slip into the room as quietly as possible, the Swami, without breaking the flow of words, would bow to me, pour me a glass of lemonade and place some sweets or a piece of fruit by my chair.

Sometimes the Swami would stroll the room while he talked. Sometimes he would sit with his eyes shut. Sometimes he would lie down on the floor. Sometimes he would stand before the picture window and look out over the desert—all the while speaking the words that were being channeled through him by some divine force.

I loved it when he lay on the floor. You could just feel the tremendous fire within him melting into the ground, as though he and the molten lava inside the earth were one. And whenever possible I would lie down next to him, so that I could melt into the earth with him.

Occasionally, I needed a nap. I would curl up on his sofa and he would put a blanket over me, then rest his hand on my head. I'd be asleep before I knew it. And while I slept, I would hear different sounds. Sometimes it would be the sound of rushing water. Sometimes it would be chimes. Sometimes it would be the wind in the willows by our pond. And sometimes it would be a sound that the Swami told me was the heart of all creation—Aum, what the Swami called "the vibration of the Cosmic Motor."

When I awoke, he might suddenly stop his dictation and say, "My prince arises. Let us take a walk." And then the two of us would tromp out into the desert.

Sometimes we wandered without saying a word. Other times we'd talk about anything that came up: cowboys, horses, pirates, some book I was reading, how the mountains were created. Whatever I was interested in, he was interested in. It sounds funny, but I felt like I was playing with my best friend—you know, a kid my own age—while also being with this wise old man who had known me forever, loved me even more than my parents did, and could teach me everything I would ever need or want to know.

I understood hardly a word the Swami spoke in his dictation sessions. I was eight, nine, ten. He was speaking the wisdom of the ages, explaining the meaning of timeless scriptures like the New Testament or the Bhagavad-Gita. Or he was speaking poetry. But while I didn't grasp the verbal concepts, what I felt always was the all-consuming love that the Swami felt for the Divine. That's all he was really doing, regardless of the words: expressing his boundless and passionate love for God. And that love showered me constantly, whether he was dictating or not.

There were times I was quite sure he fainted in the ecstasy of communion with Spirit. There were times when he would have a dialogue with Divine Mother—his consciousness in some other world, his voice speaking both parts of the conversation. And there were times when he would sit in meditation so still and without a breath for so long that I began to wonder if he had died. One time, when he'd been a rock for a couple of hours, I actually pinched his nose shut to see if he would notice, since his mouth was already closed. Nothing happened. He just sat there. My hand got tired holding his nose, that's how long it went on. I got really scared, thinking maybe I should call somebody, when all of a sudden the Swami starts laughing.

"I did the same thing to my guru once," he says, patting my cheek. "What is your diagnosis? Is the patient alive or dead?"

No matter what he was doing, I was welcome to join him. (As I say, this was quite unusual, I later learned, since he knew he was approaching the end of his life and was in seclusion, trying to finish a few things.) I have come to understand that by allowing me to be in his presence no matter what he was doing—writing a letter, giving directions to those who served him, preparing a meal—he was teaching me that any activity has meaning only by the spirit of love that infuses it. And while I may not have known what his words meant when he was dictating, I certainly felt the power of his love; such power, in fact, that I could feel it inside me, changing my body, as if turning my blood into light.

It is true that in the time we spent together during those two years, the Swami showed me many things about myself. Through him I met some of the people I've been and courageous choices I've made in former lives. Fearful choices too. The Swami also showed me unforgivenesses I still held from some of the fearful choices, and told me I would meet others as I grew up. He revealed a bit of my future, telling me about some of the people I would meet, which included some of those I had harmed in previous lives. But he never made a big deal about it. It was like he was explaining how a toy worked.

He also taught me a form of yoga meditation that is remarkably effective in awakening us to the God within, but he didn't make a big deal about that either.

And there were always numerous, fascinating anecdotes about great masters he had met. At first, I wasn't sure if he had met them in this world or some other—until he started introducing me to them, and I realized that there is no such thing as "this world" and "some other." My mother later told me that the Swami had once said to her, "Just as songs passing through the ether may be tuned in when you have a radio, so it is possible to tune in with saints, who are just behind the etheric veil of space."

Most of the time we did only everyday things, the Swami and I. I taught him how to rope a steer. He was a surprisingly good rider for a man who had seldom been on a horse. He taught me how to make various Indian foods, especially desserts. He taught me how to fold paper into any number of fierce looking birds. He knew a lot about desert plants and animals—and the name of just about every star in the sky, it seemed to me.

Shortly after we met he invited my parents and me for dinner. He had the best time introducing us to his favorite Indian dishes, which he had made himself, explaining where they originated, and what all their ingredients were, and so forth. My mother was also a very good cook, and the Swami loved Mexican food, which was one of her specialties. So, to reciprocate, she invited him to our house and prepared a banquet of her favorites. This became a ritual. We'd go to the Swami's for Indian food and he'd come to our house for Mexican. We probably had six dinners together over a period of two years. Each occasion a celebration. The Swami and my mother became so cute together. They both loved very spicy food. Whichever one of them was cooking would make one special dish that was the hottest of them all, to see if they could get the other to finally say "Uncle." At dinner, they'd each have tears streaming down their faces from the curry or cayenne or jalapeño, and yet each would say, "Oh, this is delicious," and then laugh and laugh and laugh.

During all these gatherings I don't recall that the Swami talked about God in any direct way except that, before supper and before we would part for the evening, he would say a prayer; and when he spoke, you knew he was talking to God as one speaks to a lover. And he initiated my parents to the yoga practice that he had taught me. The only other sort of 'spiritual' thing that happened was that our wolf puppy, Amigo, whose parents had been shot and we were raising for a few months, ate a prairie chicken and shards of bone got stuck in his throat and he was nearly choking to death trying to get them dislodged. The Swami rolled Amigo onto his back and scratched his belly with one hand while gently putting his other hand on the wolf's throat. Amigo immediately stopped choking and started to yowl that little yowl that all dogs have that says, You may scratch my belly for the rest of your natural life. The Swami never said a word about what he had done, but I knew what had happened, and I think my folks did, too.

As I say, I came to learn that the Swami was always teaching. And I don't mean about nature or cooking. I mean that he was always teaching me about God. No matter what he was doing (and in my presence I once heard him sharply reprimand one of the monks for not paying attention to something—and in middle of scolding the monk, the Swami turned to me and winked) he was the same: a fountain of love. That was his teaching. Do whatever you do joined with the Divine within. He was so busy with his dictation and other duties, yet he would spend as much as two or three days preparing dinner for my family, and you'd think he was doing the most important job of his life. (On his own, he would hardly eat at all, and when he did it was pretty plain.) His example is what helped me to learn that no moment or activity is more important than another: They are all opportunities to love.

One day, he told me about his mother's sudden death. He had been eleven, a year older than I at the time. He had brothers and sisters and a saintly father, but his mother's love was a universe unto itself. He hadn't known how he would live without her. Over time he came to understand that the reason his mother had been taken from him was so that he would look for solace beyond his earthly mother, finding it instead in his real mother, Divine Mother, whose presence is not circumscribed by the boundaries of life and death.

Within a month of that conversation, Lady was killed by lightning right in front of me in the desert between our ranch and the Swami's. I had been riding home in a gullywasher. I stood on Lady's steaming carcass and screamed at God, using every curse word I'd ever heard, despite not knowing the meaning of most of them. From out of storm the Swami appeared and held me, the two of us soaked to the flesh, as I wept and sank into the endlessly numbing depth of lost love for the first time in this life. Lady had been trained by my dad to be my nanny, as he put it. She'd been my closest everyday companion for five years. She had known that lightning was about to strike her, so she basically threw me, something she'd never done before, so that I would be safe when she died.

A week later, the Swami and I built a cairn to mark the place where Lady fell, then shared an apple and a carrot in her honor. It was then the Swami told me that when he left the retreat the next morning, he wouldn't be coming back. His time on earth was nearly over. He would be leaving his body within the next few days.

I was overcome with so many different emotions—about him, about Lady—that the only thing that made any sense was to hit him with all my might. Which I did, accompanied by a wail of rage and pain. I gave him a shot Rocky Marciano would have been be proud of, on the arm, just below the shoulder. Ten or not, I was a strong kid, so it hurt, I know, but the Swami didn't flinch. I, on the other hand, burst into tears. He just looked at me with all the love in the world and said, "I know."

It was my mom who later pointed out that maybe there'd been a reason why the Swami told me the story of his mother when he did.

That afternoon, the Swami and I walked a long time in silence, holding hands. By this point in his life, he didn't talk a whole lot. He was already leaving this world, I figured out later. Usually, when he was quiet I was quiet. I could tell when he was ready for me to ask him any of the many questions that were often on my mind. On this particular day, however, he was willing to talk, but I had no questions. I just wanted him. So I was rather surprised to suddenly hear myself ask him if I should join his monastic order when I grew up. As I look back on the moment today, I feel he planted the question in my mind because he knew that, eventually, I would wonder, and for some reason he wanted to give me the answer himself while he was alive.

He smiled and said, "No. That's not the path for you."

And then he said, "Very soon, one of my dearest disciples will ask me how the work I have been part of here on earth will continue without my physical presence. And I will tell that disciple something that will become the cornerstone of my teachings. I will say that when I am no longer here, only love will take my place. But even as I say it, I will know that it may take years, maybe even lifetimes, for most people, even some of my most devoted followers, to really know what 'only love' means.

"What I want you to understand, boy of my heart, is that we live in a time of tremendous ignorance on earth. You have been blessed by your devotion to Spirit in previous lives. Although you love me deeply, as I do you, we both know in our hearts that God is the only lover, and the only one loved. This Swami is no more significant in your life than a particle of dust on the moon. God is all. God is you. God is me. God is talking to God. God is listening to God.

"Most people, however, feel a need to be associated with a religion or a teacher. This is good, but only to a point. Sadly, it can be very difficult to be a member of a religious organization, or the disciple of a master, and know God. That sounds funny, doesn't it? But you see, in order to know God we must surrender everything to God, including even our attachment to our own guru and any organization associated with him. It's not enough to love a master, or even to follow a master. The goal is to become a master—a master of ourselves.

"I know this is hard for you to understand at this time. That is why, as I speak, I am also placing these words in your heart. As you get older you will be able to hear them whenever you wish and thus feel their meaning anew. I am giving you another gift, as well. You will always be able to experience that the God in me and the God in you are the same."

The Swami put his hand on my chest. "No, my sweet snake charmer, in this life your ashram is the Earth Mother. Point yourself in any direction, you'll find everything you need right here," he said, tapping my heart.

"Don't worry. If you forget, I'll remind you. It's not like I'm going anywhere."

3

The Light

SINCE WE CHOOSE our parents, I have always found it telling that I chose a father who was cremated wearing a dress and cowboy boots, and a mother who could make people nervous simply by asking them to set the dinner table.

I'd come home from school, open the hall closet to put my coat away and—surprise!—there Dad would be, standing with a big smile on his face, all dolled up: pink wig, a dress he'd bought at Goodwill for a buck, maybe an old pair of broken glasses upside down on his nose, cowboy boots of course, a cigarette stuck in each ear, lipstick, and an apron with the name Mrs. O'Flaherty embroidered across the chest. Mrs. O'Flaherty was Dad's alter ego, the lady he became whenever he cleaned the house.

"Ah, me boy," Dad would say in his phony brogue, "welcome home."

Dad had been a cowboy since before he learned to walk just about. He'd been enough of a rodeo star to sock away a nest egg. At 28 he met my mom on a Thursday and they married the following Tuesday. "Some decisions you don't have to wait on," was the way he put it. Mother's family were hand-to-mouth cattlemen, the sort of people who were just poor enough that they knew how to do just about anything. Mom and Dad spent their honeymoon buying a ranch. They went into horse training. Well, horses and anyone who worked with horses. Dad was what people today would call a horse whisperer.

"There's facts about horses, and then there's opinions," he loved to say, repeating the old saw. "If you want opinions, talk to a human; if you want the facts, talk to a horse."

Another was: "All a horse needs to learn from you is whether you can be trusted. But what you need to learn from the horse, if you really want to know a horse, is everything about yourself. And believe me, the horse can teach you that."

I remember Dad saying that about all any horse ever does is show us our fears. More than once I heard him tell someone not to ride for a while, and this might be someone who'd been riding all their life.

"Right now, you hate fear," he'd say, "which means you hate everything that might cause fear, which means you hate everything—since every moment is full of the unknown and potential catastrophe. A person who hates fear can only harm a horse. No horse deserves that."

He didn't ask people to be unafraid, since everyone has fear. But his work began with helping people learn how to manage fear, developing inner skills so that fear became their friend—not just something they could tolerate, but something they loved. "Fear is always showing us where we need to surrender in order to be one with a horse," Dad would say, "which really means being one with our self."

Our ranch was named Egolightly. "The price for being a good horse handler is having to wear your ego lightly," Dad said. "Your strong beliefs, no matter what they are, are as tough on a horse as a saddle that doesn't fit."

It got to be very amusing. People who didn't know a horse from a water buffalo would call or write and ask if they could work with Dad—and these were people who had no intention of ever riding. They just wanted to work with the man who had had such an impact on some friend of theirs.

Just as Dad had his special ways of teaching, so did Mother.

She would go to auctions and antique shops and deliberately buy just one of something in a particular pattern. They were all very nice pieces, but as a collection they were just all different. Our kitchen was like a museum, only we used everything. Mom never really made a big deal of it. She just did it. And she did it to remind all of us, which included the never-ending stream of guests, that we're always making choices.

At our house, you made yourself a bowl of cereal, and not only did you get to choose the cereal, you had to choose the bowl and the spoon...or not choose it, at least consciously, as you preferred. You could just take whatever came naturally to your hand when you reached into the cupboard or drawer—discovering what gift the universe had for you in that moment.

Mom would almost always ask a guest to set the table for dinner. And of course the person would say, "Oh, I'd be happy to." But then, when they learned what they were really being asked to do, sometimes you'd sense this small "gulp."

And it wasn't just the silver and china and napkins and drinking glasses that you had to choose and arrange however you liked. You could add flowers from the garden and candles and anything else you could think of. Put a little poem on everybody's plate if you felt moved to do it. Have anyone sit in whatever seat you chose. That was often a tough one. People were always asking Mom, "Where does so-and-so sit?" and Mom would say, "Wherever you say, dear. The table is yours to create."

The only guiding principle besides 'follow your heart' was that you were informed what we were having for dinner—Mom's way of teaching the importance of being aware of what this very moment is asking.

No matter how you set the table, there was always a big celebration about it.

When the Swami came to dinner, things got really wild. He insisted on setting the table. He was like a kid. One time he had us eating our soup while riding backward and bareback on a horse, a placemat laid over the horse's rump. And that wasn't all of it. Everything was always very orderly on the ranch. Things had their place. But before dinner the Swami engaged in a little mischievous rearranging. A rope, for example, that always hung on a certain hook, he took off the hook and laid it on the ground. That sort of thing. The game he made up was that we were to eat our soup without spilling any, at the same time we were to spot how many items were not where they were supposed to be. It was actually rather difficult because no one could stop laughing.

Later, the Swami told us the story of an Indian king who trains a young prince by having him walk through the castle with a lamp that is full to the brim with oil. The prince's task is to notice everything he encounters but not spill a drop of the oil—so that he can answer any question about his journey the king might ask him.

During the time we knew the Swami my father had three birthdays. Each birthday the Swami gave my father the same present: a bushel of ordinary light bulbs. Dad used to say that under all the silly ways we humans behave we're all just shiny balls of light. We just don't know it.

The Swami's gift inspired Dad to start a tradition of his own. Whenever the spirit moved him, he would give someone—often a child—a beautifully wrapped box inside of which, cushioned in gold tissue, was one of the Swami's light bulbs.

Dad never explained that his gift had originally come from the Swami because sometimes, after receiving the bulbs, people's lives changed rather dramatically. An illness would suddenly disappear. A kid's parent would find a job. In one case, life-long depression went away. Dad preferred that people not make the connection between the light bulb and whatever blessing they received. That would have been a distraction. To Dad, all that mattered was the reminder of who we really are.

I was well over 60 when my father died. It was his 100th birthday. For as long as I can recall, Dad told the story that when he was five, God told him to pick a number from 10 to 100. For what reason, Dad didn't know, or at least never said. Anyway, Dad picked the number 100 because it was bigger than anything he could imagine, the closest thing to God himself. But then, as Dad's life went on, he came to learn that the numeral "1" actually represents God, the big One—and it also represents the sun, a big shiny ball of light.

None of us suspected that Dad might die on his birthday. It wasn't something he advertised. And he was certainly sparkly enough for a man of his years. As always, his birthday breakfast was chocolate cake. "Plan for the unexpected. Start the day with dessert," was one of Dad's mottos. Then he said, as he often did, "I'm just going to take a little nap," and he simply never woke up.

At his memorial, when I got up to say a few words, the first thing I did was pull out of my pocket, and hold up for everyone to see, the light bulb Dad had given me for my eleventh birthday, my first birthday after the Swami died.

Then the most amazing thing happened. Just about everyone there reached into their pocket and pulled out the light bulb they had brought with them—and held it up. At that moment we all realized that this wasn't something anybody had planned. No notice had gone out: "Please bring your light bulb." It just happened. Some of these people had traveled long distances, not having seen my dad in years. Many of them weren't even the original recipients of Dad's gift; they were the recipient's children.

Standing there in rather awed silence, our light bulbs raised like so many statues of liberty, we found ourselves weeping for reasons we might never be able to fully explain.

As I looked around the gathering, did I really see the better part of two bushels worth of light bulbs floating overhead, glowing ever so softly? It makes a nice story, but all I can say for sure is what I felt: the love I had first experienced well over a half-century earlier on that afternoon when the Swami said to me, "So, we meet again."

THE MAKING OF
ST. PORCINE

A man does not have to be an angel
in order to be a saint.

—*Albert Schweitzer*

IT IS FITTING THAT MY NAME in that life was Abraham. It has a rather kingly ring, and I was nothing if not regal. I was the abbot. I ran a monastery. My wavy hair was bleached and trained to resemble rays of the sun haloing my face. I was the benevolent shepherd, God's perfection my only desire. Perfect beauty. Perfect humility. Perfect harmony. And because righteousness was my middle name, I was not above murder to achieve my ends.

I've seen only a handful of movies. One of them, "Saving Private Ryan," contains a scene where a German soldier and an American soldier are fighting to the death, hand-to-hand. They're in a small room, a bedroom maybe, on an upper floor of a mostly bombed-out apartment building. The German has a knife and, after a protracted clash of men doing everything they know how to stay alive, the German (a few more incarnations as a warrior under his belt) is able to insert the tip of his knife at the American's solar plexus and slowly, against the American's great resistance of the impending reality, push the blade upward into the American's heart. In that final struggle, the German lay atop the American like a lover, their breaths entwined as well as their bodies. That sense of intimacy, tenderness even, yet ultimate dominance by the more seasoned man, was one of the threads of my relationship with the monks I led.

My right hand in that life was a young monk I shall name Brother Moon, since I shaped him to be a reflection of me, or at least

188

the reflection that suited my ends. He took over as abbot upon my death, permitting me to rule from the grave.

How unspecial this story is—fear preferred to love.

Certain spiritual practices result in a greater than everyday ability to manipulate the physical universe. My best trick was offering you a bowl of fruit that, no matter how much of it you ate, always remained full. My faculties, exhibited judiciously, inspired awe far beyond our cloister walls. Many considered me a saint, or something close. They failed to realize that flashy powers and knowing God are two completely different things.

It is comical in hindsight. I worked for years developing the ability to create fruit at will, ignoring the fact that, thanks to the heavenly grocer, it would have taken a lot less energy to simply go to the market.

A young boy came to our abbey. Let's call him William, as in conqueror. He might have been 13. He knew God. I should have been touching his feet, so pure in spirit was even the way he wiped his nose.

A quivering dog in a lightning storm, that was me in the face of all I would need to relinquish in order to know the divine as William did. And much worse, my disciples would realize just how un-saintly I was.

Ah, but still, I was Abraham. I would never toss a supplicant into the street. Instead, I created the circumstances in which William would choose to leave on his own or (like many before him, though none so innocent) be destroyed.

It was neither difficult nor obvious. In my monastery there was a right way to do everything. Rules were clear, enforcement strict. William couldn't be bothered. He didn't dismiss rules; he just never considered them. It was like teaching a chicken to bake a cake. Maybe harder. But there were no exceptions to my commandments, and so William was in a state of continual reprimand, each one a little more fierce than the last.

He didn't mind. He was a boy who, if you told him he was so useless that it would take him a million years to know God, would dance with joy that tomorrow he would be one day closer.

William wasn't the first to be banished to the outdoors in winter, but he was the first who chose to live on his knees at the ocean's edge. He died an ice sculpture. A praying angel.

On the day he was buried, William's spirit appeared to me, thanking me for giving him so many opportunities to surrender himself to God. Without me, he said, he might not have experienced the sacred presence in this lifetime, and that I, therefore, was a great soul. He said that he would do whatever he could to inflame hearts everywhere to seek God through me.

I whimpered.

That night, lit by stars on snow, I and my protégé dug up William's casket, hacked his corpse into small pieces, and fed the morsels to our pigs: an Inquisitional ritual of ultimate revilement—casting a soul into a thousand-year wasteland devoid of contact with beings in any form. My spin to Brother Moon was that William had always been possessed, and that I had kept him with us in the prayer that God's grace would work a miracle. But alas... That was why William was unable to follow even the simplest direction. And why the devil had been able to seduce William into believing that winter was summer.

How easy it is to lie when one lives with internal panic and the awe of those around him.

But William's spirit transcended ceremony. Again he appeared, prostrate, thanking me over and over, saying how I had helped him give up his last remaining attachment to himself as a physical being. And again he said I was a great soul, and again he said that seekers for generations to come would be drawn to God through me.

I shared none of this with Brother Moon, to be sure.

I had a nightmare. My monks ate the pigs. The spirit of William entered them. Infused with the divine, not one revered me anymore. So I ordered the pigs sold to an itinerant butcher whose route wouldn't bring him within a league of my monastery for many months.

The visits from William stopped. We bought new piglets. Life returned to normal.

Until, that is, a breeze started to blow that miracles were occurring throughout the land. Blindness, palsy, hunchback, whatever... Cured.

Such things happened on occasion. Always they were investigated, and almost always were found to be the work of the devil. Anything the church couldn't take credit for it condemned. Execution by fire was the most painless penalty. As expected, Lord Poobah (we'll call him), master of the realm, ordered an inquiry and, also as expected, enlisted the most revered person in the land to supervise it: Moi.

Naturally, each miracle recipient had eaten bacon or chops, hocks or a pickled foot procured from one itinerant butcher.

"But Abbot, what will you tell Lord Poobah?" Brother Moon asked, fearing what might be revealed about the diet of these miraculous porkers. Foolish boy.

"I shall tell him the truth, my son. Those pigs came from our cloister. Everything else is irrelevant."

And so, by murdering and defiling the saintliest person I knew and lying about it, I became even more venerated, just as William had predicted. And the more venerated I became, and the more postulants joined our brotherhood, the more I quivered in my private moments. My fear wasn't that the truth about William would be revealed. It was that the truth about me would be revealed—my addiction to being thought of as holy.

My powers allowed me to contract pneumonia the following winter, and after I died my monks and other believers pestered Rome for my beatification as the saint who used the common pig to work miracles—as I, of course, knew they would.

It is amusing and painful to imagine myself as St. Porcine. For centuries butchers and pig farmers praying to me, yet here I am still forgiving myself for the devastation I created in fear all those lifetimes ago. I have a lot of empathy for tyrants, from turf-hoarding bureaucrats, to wife beaters, to genocidal maniacs bent on destroying an entire people. I've been given the questionable gift of appreciating in ways that span incarnations that, when we live in fear, all bets are off—harm is the only sure thing.

William visits from time to time. Still supporting me how many incarnations later.

Usually we simply embrace in the sanctuary of the unconditional, but there are occasions when I might be taking myself a tad too seriously, at which he is not above bringing me to my senses by asking, "Care for a ham sandwich, Abe?"

One time he tisked: "Oh, you poor boy. You have nobody to kill this time around but yourself."

Dying to life through forgiveness.

EPILOGUE

The universe, you may have noticed,
can be irritatingly supportive.

SHORTLY AFTER MOVING to Vermont and turning 50, both within a month's time, I developed this itch to do something completely unprecedented—get a vanity license plate. The universe (in its usual playful way) was once again prodding me to go deep, this time by distilling my spirit to a single burp of seven letters or fewer.

Still, I'm nothing if not pretentious. Since I've always been drawn to the essence of things ("What is air in this situation, what can we not live without?"), I wanted the statement on my plate to be the single most potent word in all of language—I mean, *any* language, at any time, in the history of the world. If you had to choose one word to express the heart of existence—the force that impels the evolution of humankind—what would that word be? That's what I asked myself. And curiously enough, the answer arrived in about the time it takes to smile.

"Yess!"

We're all familiar with that juicy, emphatic "Yess!" It's the price of admission to the life we want. Only when we say "Yess!" to the astonishing array of possibility inherent in whatever our moments present do we tap into ourselves at our best.

Of course it's not the easiest choice to make, because the "Yess!" I'm talking about comes only from our heart, the voice of our true self that unerringly leads in the direction of kindness, even though the route may more than occasionally oblige us to tiptoe across a carpet of alligators before jumping off a cliff.

At least that's been my experience. Then again, before I was born, I evidently asked for whatever life circumstances would help me most to know the real me. Maybe that's why my first career aspiration was saint. That and cowboy seemed like about the most fun a person could have. As far back as I can remember, the universe has given me both unconditional loving support and increasingly uncompromising requests to live from my heart or die. If I ever thought that moving to lovely Vermont and turning 50 would somehow bring a certain tranquility to this process, that delusion went poof soon after I adorned my sedan with "the world's most powerful license plate."

I remember the exact moment. I had just walked onto this farm and knew instantly that it was to be my home.

Oh, the universe was really yucking it up that day, for buying and maintaining a huge farm meant that I would have to generate much more income than I had ever intended.

Actually, I'm one of the wealthiest people on earth. Just not when it comes to money. My wealth has always been the more intangible variety, measured in the freedom to spend my time as I wish, getting paid for doing things I would do even if I didn't get paid. Purchasing this farm could change all that, I trembled. I might have to put making a living before indulging my whim. Maybe even get a job. Not a pretty picture for a man who'd worked for himself just long enough to be virtually unemployable. I'm making light of it now, but at the time my funny bone had been misplaced where the sun don't shine. For weeks my anguish mounted, me nursing my fear. Then came the morning I was snowshoeing alone in the Green Mountain National Forest, hours from anywhere, immersed in that absolute silence that occurs only in the dead of winter, when in a spasm of self-pity I start quacking to the sky: "Come on, I need help here. What am I going to do?"

You know what they say: When you talk to God, it's prayer. When God talks to you, it's schizophrenia.

"Oh, shut up," said the voice of my heart. "Quit whining. Buy the farm. And do it with a positive attitude."

Needless to say, I was a bit startled. I like to think I'm as connected to the Almighty as the next guy, but seldom have I been spoken to so forcefully. Usually it's more of a suggestion. So I did what any sensible person would do. I snowshoed back the next day and said, "Lord, was that you? Or was that my imagination?"

Again, instantly, I heard the voice of my heart issuing the same directive: "Shut up. Quit whining. Buy the farm. And do it with a positive attitude."

So, somehow, and I can't really tell you how, I did. I shifted. I let go of fear. I made room for abundance.

In other words, I said "Yess!"

Within days, it seems, the phone started ringing. People I'd never heard of were saying, "We got your name from so-and-so, and were wondering if you could help us out."

If Brinks had backed a dump truck to my office door and yelled "Delivery!" I couldn't have been more amazed. And humbled, frankly, since I was being reminded that just maybe the universe knew more about running my life than I did.

"It wouldn't hurt you to trust a little," said the voice of my heart. "You think you were given that license plate by accident?"

This phase of worldly activity lasted about five years, when another whisper started getting on my nerves: "Give up all your professional work and write."

Do you know what the prospects are for writers whose careers begin in their 50s? Only slightly better than Pavarotti becoming a jockey. And it wasn't like the farm and all its needs had vanished. Plus, I was making a good living. So, I did what any sensible person would do when it came to my inner voice on this particular topic. I ignored it.

The universe, you may have noticed, can be irritatingly supportive. Any time we don't listen to its gentle reminders, we're given reminders that are increasingly less gentle, until, if we persist in our claim that denial is a river in

Egypt, a giant tomato tossed off a 10 story building has our name on it (whatever it takes for us to make the move that will serve our heart's desire to love ever more robustly)—the Great Ones standing on the sidelines, tee-hee-ing, shaking their tambourines.

Which is how it happened that after I'd kept my head in the sand for a good year, the Brinks guys simply stopped showing up. People who had once said I was the answer to their prayers now said it was time for a change.

"What did you expect?" said the voice of my heart. "Either you take action, or we'll take it for you. It's time for you to offer yourself to the world in new ways."

Despite my resistance, I was glad for the shove. I knew I'd been chicken. Besides, I rationalized, I was already a pretty fair advertising writer. How difficult could fiction or essays be? Even legendary sportswriter Red Smith said putting words on paper wasn't all that tough. All you had to do was sit down at the typewriter and open up a vein.

My office used to be so tidy. Now there's blood all over the place.

Don't plan, don't strategize, and for crying out loud don't think, said the voice of my heart. When we want your opinion we'll give it to you. Just show up, sit your fanny at the keyboard, and go within. Keep those fingers moving. Be playful. Generosity begins by enjoying yourself. Breathe through your fear of being broke and homeless. What's the Steinbeck line—It's one thing to be able to write, another to have something to say? Quit being afraid to find out that you don't have much to offer on either score. Are we hurting your little feelings? Then get big feelings!

Writing, as you can tell, wasn't the point. Writing was just the teacher. And one that showed up every day with a whoopee cushion and a bullwhip. At first I felt sorry for myself that I didn't have Johnny Irving as my next-door neighbor so I could run over every ten minutes and say what do you think of this. Soon, though, I discovered that the guidance I needed most was already sitting next to me—

in an old journal where I found a saying of the Buddha that, since high school, has been a benevolent, if dogged, presence:

Do not believe anything on mere hearsay; do not believe traditions because they are old and handed down through many generations; do not believe simply because the written testimony of some ancient sage is shown to you; never believe anything because presumption is in its favor or the custom of many years leads you to regard it as true; do not believe anything on the mere authority of teachers or priests. Whatever according to your own experiences and after thorough investigation agrees with your reason, and is conducive to your own weal and to that of all other living things, <u>that</u> accept as truth and live accordingly.

Now here we are, four years later—and I feel like the boy who met the wolfhound of compassion. The wolfhound invites the boy to hop on its back and travel to lands that will give the boy a chance to make friends with the person he fears the most—himself, as it turns out—then share that friendship with anyone who can use it. The journey isn't new. Only the traveling companion is. The journey is one we're all making.

This is the point where the violins come in and I tell you that I'm actually becoming play-mates with those ghosts named Penniless, Homeless and Toothless. Oh sure, I still let my-self be terrorized by them on occasion, but I'm grateful (usually) for all they teach me. More-over, I've got my bride, my dog, and I'm fol-lowing my bliss, laptop under my arm. See me strolling toward a windswept cliff overlooking the ocean and the rising sun.

Only, upon closer inspection, you'll notice that I am actually tiptoeing across a carpet of alligators, for not too long ago the voice of my heart started whispering, "Yoo-hoo."

ACKNOWLEDGEMENTS

*They say a man whose fly is open all day
doesn't have enough friends.*

M Y FATHER TOLD ME that before I was
born he got down on his knees and
prayed for a son. It was a blessing to grow up
knowing I was a gift from God, never mind
that my pop might have had second thoughts
about his request when it became clear that I
arrived with a mind of my own. Both my parents told me regularly that I could do anything.
So when I think about acknowledging those
who have helped to bring forward the me that
lives in these pages I must begin with Philadel-
phia Bill Crissy and his bride Shorty Scarbor-

ough. If there's a bookstore in heaven, I'm sure they're pushing this little baby on everyone they meet.

Then there is my guru, the avatar Parama-hansa Yogananda. When we met (so to speak, since it was some 30 years after he died) I said, "I refuse to take anything on faith." He laughed. "Why would you? All I ask is that you try what I suggest with an open heart. Keep what works. And don't kid yourself." I don't think anyone has ever made me a better offer.

I live with five other adults on a 200-acre mountainside retreat. Ours is what you might call an "intentional" community, our intention being to grow our capacity to love. There are times when blindfolded brain surgery would be easier, but never would it be more reward-ing. In more ways than I'm aware, my life is shaped by this family of the heart: Frogman, Noni, Chris, Ifetayo, and Dear, my one true love.

They say a man whose fly is open all day doesn't have enough friends. I'm not sure what to make of the fact that it has taken all the people I'm about to mention (and plenty more) to keep me even reasonably zipped as a human being, much less as a writer: Boston Globe Bill Waldron; Racy Rita Ring; Jane Yolen; Tom Jenks; Charlotte Fitzpatrick; Long Island Pete; Santa Fe Susan; Captain Herb Gross; Paul Donuts Coon; Scotty Kielbasa; Odds Bodkin; jazzman Tommy Rizzo; Kim Townsend; Conge & Sue; Doug McLaine; John Boy Kring and Sue Shapiro; Janet McKenzie; Audrey Saphar; Peter Millard; David Wolpe; Jeffery Schoening; Susan Free Press Reid (who was first to publish some of the essays in this collection); Rob Wallace; Jan Stuart; M.D. Thew, MD; John Ewing; Ian Wilson; Violin Julie Gigante; Maple Dave Marvin; Craftsbury Dave Stember; Minnesota Dave Hammel; Elmira Carl Proper; my siblings Georgia, Rob and Cris Crissy; Terrie Gottstein; Newcomb Greenleaf; Al Q-Man Kao; Charissa Rigano; Rich Hyde; Harry Beagle; Butch Bauer; Big Ed Wall; Heidi Hall; Joey Callan; Josie Estill; Bonnie Skakel; Jamey Stillings; Jeff Moores; Michael Jager; Jack Slagle; Steve Haefele; Joyce Stember; Brad Smith; Wayne Calabrese; Kent Mitchell; Mary McIsaac; Simon Kahn; Carla

Kelley; Craig Neal; Sally Stetson; Lynn Wood; Doug Harp; Dick Henry; Carol Hanley; Joe Sherman; Josephine Spilka; Paul Suhadolc; the offspring of my heart: Peter, Kathryn and Simone; guys with funny names like Atmananda, Chidananda, Devananda, Jayananda, Mitrananda, Sevananda and Vishwananda; not to mention the beautiful Daya Mata—and I'm just warming up.

Put all these folks in the same room and ask them to set the world's agenda for the next millennium and never again will you doubt the power, beauty and ingenuity of the human spirit. Each one of them has enriched my life, many by telling me I was full of crap. Isn't it astonishing how we get puffed up thinking that we, on our own, have ever achieved anything?

And then there are the heavyweights, those teachers whose mere presence reminds us all that every choice reverberates for generations. I am speaking of the children: Queen Isabella; Dr. Factual J. Johnson; Sammy Starwalker; Rachel, William, Elizabeth, Caroline and Jordan; Robert and Morgan; Seneca; Owen and Fiona; Zoe and Mia; Sydney; Maggie and Ian; Ananda Joy and Zeena Padme; Sam and Theo; Aquene and Rec; Hannah; Evie Grace and Wyatt; and Zoe River.

Here's how the universe works: For years I've sort of half rolled my eyes when I hear some author rhapsodizing about the blah-blah-blah of his or her editor. To be sure, having never worked with an editor my blasé has been unencumbered by experience. Today the Great Ones are still slapping their thighs after introducing me to Cathy Dees and watching the delightful impact her sniper's eye and saint's heart has had on me and this offering.

Finally, every business is somebody's baby, and so St. Lynn's Press is Paul Kelly's. Perhaps especially so right now since this book is among St. Lynn's first. It takes a lot of guts to ask an unknown schmoe to carry the spirit of your baby into the world. I, the schmoe in question, bow to Mr. Kelly in gratitude.

CREDITS

Editor:
Cathy Dees
stlynnspress.com

Cover Design:
Sally Stetson
SallyStetsonDesign.com

Interior Design:
Georgia Dent
MonkfishPublishing.com

Cover Photo:
Jerome Johnson
EarthandSpirit.com

Author Photo:
Wayne Calabrese
Coupdetat.com

Scupture Photos:
Steve Roberts
CoolMindWarmHeart.com

ABOUT THE AUTHOR

Steve Roberts lives, writes, counsels and builds stone sculptures on a Vermont mountainside. He is a strategist and mentor, helping leaders gain clarity on what is essential—particularly in painful times. He is also a ghostwriter of memoirs, and his essays appear regularly in The Burlington Free Press. Steve serves those who know a most remarkable thing about themselves: They are not remotely who they think they are. None of us are. None of us are that small. Our capacity for self-discovery is immeasurable.

Steve can be found on the web at:
CoolMindWarmHeart.com*.*

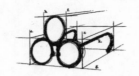